Shining Star A

Anna Uhl Chamot

Pamela Hartmann

Jann Huizenga

Longman

longman.com

Shining Star

Pearson Education, 10 Bank Street, White Plains, NY 10606

Vice president, director of instructional design: Allen Ascher
Editorial director: Ed Lamprich
Acquisitions editor: Amanda Rappaport Dobbins
Project manager: Susan Saslow
Senior development editors: Virginia Bernard, Bill Preston
Vice president, director of design and production: Rhea Banker
Executive managing editor: Linda Moser
Production manager: Ray Keating
Senior production editor: Sylvia Dare
Production editor: Patricia W. Nelson
Director of manufacturing: Patrice Fraccio
Senior manufacturing buyer: Edith Pullman
Photo research: Kirchoff/Wohlberg, Inc.
Design and production: Kirchoff/Wohlberg, Inc.
Cover design: Rhea Banker, Tara Mayer
Text font: 12.5/16 Minion
Acknowledgments: See page 278.
Illustration and photo credits: See page 279.

Library of Congress Cataloging-in-Publication Data
Chamot, Anna Uhl.
  Shining star / Anna Uhl Chamot, Pamela Hartmann, Jann Huizenga.
    p. cm.
  Includes index.
  Contents: A. Level 1. — B. Level 2. — C. Level 3.
  ISBN 0-13-093931-5 (pt. A) — ISBN 0-13-093933-1 (pt. B) — ISBN
0-13-093934-X (pt. C)
  1. English language—Textbooks for foreign speakers. [1. English
language—Textbooks for foreign speakers. 2. Readers.] I. Hartmann,
Pamela. II Huizenga, Jann. III. Title.

PE1128.C48 2003
428.2'4—dc21

                                                    2002043460

ISBN: 0-13-093931-5

Printed in the United States of America
1 2 3 4 5 6 7 8 9 10–RRD–08 07 06 05 04 03

About the Authors

Anna Uhl Chamot is professor of secondary education and faculty adviser for ESL in George Washington University's Department of Teacher Preparation. She has been a researcher and teacher trainer in content-based second-language learning and language-learning strategies. She codesigned and has written extensively about the

Cognitive Academic Language Learning Approach (CALLA) and spent seven years implementing the CALLA model in the Arlington Public Schools in Virginia.

Pamela Hartmann is a teacher and writer in the field of Teaching English to Speakers of Other Languages (TESOL). She has taught ESL and EFL in California and overseas since 1973. In addition, she has authored several books in the fields of TESOL and cross-cultural communication.

Jann Huizenga is an educator and consultant in the field of TESOL, with a special interest in teaching reading. She has worked as a teacher trainer at Hunter College in New York City, at the University of New Mexico at Los Alamos, and overseas. She has written numerous books for ESL students.

Consultants and Reviewers

Jennifer Alexander
Houston ISD
Houston, Texas

Heidi Ballard
University of California at Berkeley
Henry M. Gunn High School
Palo Alto, California

Susan Benz
Balboa High School
San Francisco, California

Lynore M. Carnuccio
esl, etc Educational Consultants
Yukon, Oklahoma

Wes Clarkson
El Paso ISD
El Paso, Texas

Lynn Clausen
Pajaro Valley USD
Watsonville, California

Brigitte Deyle
Northside ISD
San Antonio, Texas

Janet L. Downey
Riverside Unified School District
Riverside, California

Elvira Estrada
Socorro ISD
El Paso County, Texas

Virginia L. Flanagin
University of California at Berkeley
Berkeley, California

Leanna Harrison
Stinson Middle School
San Antonio, Texas

Gloria Henllan-Jones
Amundsen High School
Chicago, Illinois

Ann Hilborn
Educational Consultant
Houston, Texas

Terry Hirsch
Waukegan High School
Waukegan, Illinois

Kevin Kubota
Freeman High School
Richmond, Virginia

Betsy Lewis-Moreno
Thomas Edison High School
San Antonio, Texas

Caroline LoBuglio
Lower East Side Preparatory High
  School
New York, New York

Jean McConochie
Pace University
New York, New York

James McGuinness
National Faculty – Lesley University
Yarmouthport, Massachusetts

Kaye Wiley Maggart
New Haven Public Schools
New Haven, Connecticut

Maria Malagon
Montgomery County Public Schools
Rockville, Maryland

Elva Ramirez Mellor
Chula Vista Elementary School
  District
Chula Vista, California

Wendy Meyers
Casey Middle School
Boulder, Colorado

Linda Nelson
Century High School
Santa Ana, California

Jessica O'Donovan
Bilingual/ESL Technical Assistance
  Center (BETAC)
Elmsford, New York

Patrizia Panella
Isaac E. Young Middle School
New Rochelle, New York

Kathy Privrat
Lower East Side Preparatory
  High School
New York, New York

Jan Reed
Garden Grove USD
Garden Grove, California

Leslie S. Remington
Hermitage High School
Richmond, Virginia

Linda Riehl
Grady Middle School
Houston, Texas

Michael Ringler
Hialeah-Miami Lakes Senior
  High School
Hialeah, Florida

Alma Rodriguez
Bowie High School
El Paso, Texas

Marjorie Bandler Rosenberg
Malrose Associates
Annandale, Virginia

Sandra Salas
Rayburn Middle School
San Antonio, Texas

Carrie Schreiber
International Newcomer
  Academy
Fort Worth, Texas

Angela Seale
Independent Consultant
Houston, Texas

Penny Shanihan
Pearland High School
Houston, Texas

Katherine Silva
Holmes High School
San Antonio, Texas

Kathleen Anderson Steeves
The George Washington
  University
Washington, D.C.

Trudy Todd
Fairfax Public Schools,
  Emeritus
Fairfax County, Virginia

Sylvia Velasquez
Braddock Senior High School
Miami, Florida

Sharon Weiss
Educational Consultant
Glenview, Illinois

Ruth White
Washington High School
Cedar Rapids, Iowa

To the Student

Welcome to

Shining Star

This program will help you develop the English skills you need for different school subjects. Each unit has selections about a variety of topics, including science, social studies, and math. There are also literary selections. These selections will help you understand the vocabulary and organization of different types of texts such as stories, poems, and nonfiction articles. They will give you the tools you need to approach the content of the different subjects you take in school.

Before starting to read a selection, you will do activities that help you relate your background knowledge to the new information in the text. You will also study some of the new words in the text to give you a head start as you begin to read. Finally, you will learn a reading strategy that will help you read with greater understanding.

While you read, ask yourself, "Am I understanding this? Does it make sense to me?" Remember to use the reading strategy! Your teacher may also play a recording of the selection so that you can listen to it as you read.

After you read, you will check your understanding of the text. Then you will work on activities to help improve your English skills in grammar, phonics, and spelling.

To extend your ability in English, you will participate in several types of activities related to the selections in each unit. Some of these activities involve listening and speaking, while in others you will produce different kinds of writing. Each unit also has a number of projects in which you can practice your artistic, musical, dramatic, scientific, mathematical, language, social, and thinking talents. You'll also see some suggestions for further reading related to the theme of the unit.

We hope that you enjoy *Shining Star* as much as we enjoyed writing it for you!

Anna Uhl Chamot
Pamela Hartmann
Jann Huizenga

Contents

PART 2

PUT IT ALL TOGETHER

UNIT 2

Challenges and Choices

PART 2

PUT IT ALL TOGETHER

Mysterious Ways

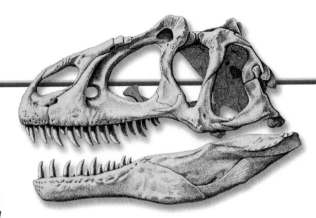

PART 2

PUT IT ALL TOGETHER

UNIT 4

Conflict

PART 2

PUT IT ALL TOGETHER

UNIT 5

We Can Be Heroes

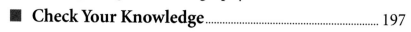

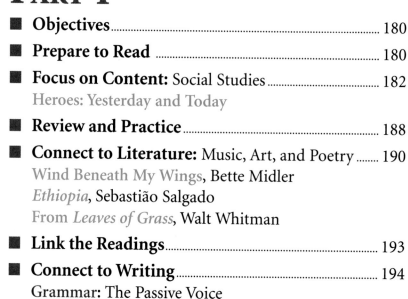

PART 2

PUT IT ALL TOGETHER

UNIT 6

Look Into the Future 222

PART 1

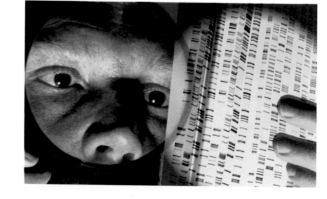

PART 2

PUT IT ALL TOGETHER

Growing Up

2

PART 1

- "Ancient Kids"
- "The Hare and the Tortoise," Aesop
- "Why Rattlesnake Has Fangs," Cheryl Giff

PART 2

- From *Later, Gator*, Laurence Yep
- "Amazing Growth Facts"

Growing up can mean many things. Babies and children grow up as they get bigger and their bodies change. Changing the way we think and act can also be growing up. We grow up as we learn from our experiences and accept more responsibility.

In Part 1, you will read an informational text about growing up in three ancient cultures. You will also read two stories—a fable and a myth. Each story describes an experience that helps someone learn something or change in some way.

In Part 2, you will read an excerpt from a novel. The novel is about two brothers. The older brother has many negative feelings about his younger brother. You will see some ways that the younger brother can help the older brother grow up. Finally, you will read an informational text about ways some plants and animals grow.

3

PART 1

Prepare to Read

OBJECTIVES

LANGUAGE DEVELOPMENT

Reading:
- Vocabulary building: *Context, dictionary skills*
- Reading strategy: *Previewing*
- Text types: *Social studies text, fable, myth*
- Literary element: *Personification*

Writing:
- Descriptive writing
- Sentences
- Word web
- Editing checklist

Listening/Speaking:
- Appreciation: *fable, myth*
- Culture: *Connecting experiences*
- Compare and contrast characters
- Retell a fable or myth

Grammar:
- Adjectives

Viewing/Representing:
- Timelines, diagrams, charts

ACADEMIC CONTENT
- Social studies vocabulary
- Ancient Greek, Roman, Maya cultures

BACKGROUND

"Ancient Kids" is an informational text about three ancient cultures. It is a nonfiction text. That means it is about real facts or events. The purpose of an informational text is to inform the reader about real facts, people, or events.

Kids in ancient cultures had different experiences from kids today. However, there are also some similarities.

Make connections Think about yourself now and when you were younger. Use this timeline to help you remember. Look at the timeline and think about your life. Discuss the questions in pairs. (For some questions, you can point to the timeline as you answer.)

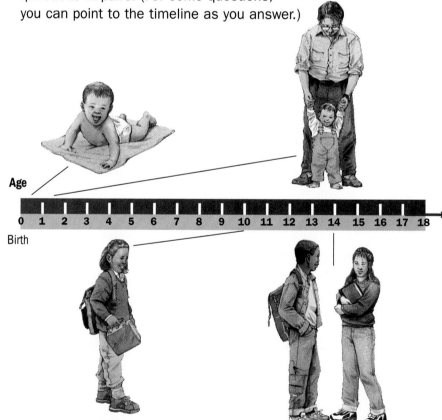

Age

0 1 2 3 4 5 6 7 8 9 10 11 12 13 14 15 16 17 18

Birth

1. What year were you born?
2. How old were you when you started school?
3. What toys did you play with when you were younger? What games or sports did you play?
4. How old are you now?

VOCABULARY

LEARN KEY WORDS

ancient
ceremony
citizen
cultures
education
rights

Sometimes you can guess what a new word means from the sentence it is in. This is called guessing from context. Read these sentences. Use the context to figure out the meaning of the **red** words. Use a dictionary to check your answers. Write each word and its meaning in your notebook.

1. Rome is an **ancient** city. It is thousands of years old.
2. The Maya had a **ceremony** to mark the end of childhood, when children turned twelve or thirteen.
3. If you are not a **citizen** of Mexico, you cannot vote there.
4. Different **cultures** often have different beliefs, customs, and ways of life.
5. We get our **education** both in school and at home.
6. Americans have many **rights**. For example, the law allows Americans to speak freely.

READING STRATEGY

Previewing

Previewing helps you understand a text. Before you read:

- look at the **title**
- look for **headings** (titles of the different sections of the text)
- look at the **photographs** and **illustrations**.

Think about the information you got from the title, headings, and photographs and illustrations. Try to establish your reasons for reading the text.

title

headings → What is the text about?

photographs and illustrations

5

Social Studies

ANCIENT KIDS
GROWING UP IN ANCIENT GREECE

ANCIENT GREECE

| 2000 B.C.E | 323 B.C.E | 0 | 2000 C.E. |

When a baby was born in ancient Greece, the father did a **ritual** dance, holding the newborn baby. For boy babies, the family decorated the house with **wreaths** of olives. For girl babies, the family decorated the house with wreaths made of wool.

There were many differences in the lives of boys and girls as they grew up. One main difference was that girls did not go to school and boys did. Some girls learned to play musical instruments.

Mostly, girls helped their mothers with **chores** in the house or in the fields. They didn't leave their houses very often. Sometimes they went to festivals or funerals. They also visited neighbors.

Girls stayed home with their parents until they got married. Girls' fathers usually decided who they would marry.

Boys stayed home until they were six or seven years old. They helped grow **crops** in the fields, and they learned to sail boats and to fish.

▲ Some girls learned to read and write at home.

---

ritual, based on religious rules
wreaths, decorative circles made of flowers, plants, or other items
chores, small jobs
crops, wheat, corn, fruit, etc., that a farmer grows

When boys were about seven years old, they started their formal education. They went to school and learned reading, writing, and mathematics. They had to **memorize** everything because there were no school books! They memorized the poetry of Homer, a famous poet. They also learned to play a musical instrument, such as a **lyre.**

At school, boys learned about the arts and war. They also learned how to be good citizens. At the age of eighteen, boys went to **military school** for two years.

Children played with many toys, such as rattles, clay animals, pull-toys on four wheels, yo-yos, and **terra-cotta** dolls. Children also had pets, such as birds, dogs, goats, tortoises, and mice.

▲ A student and his teacher working together

---

memorize, remember the exact words
lyre, ancient instrument, similar to a guitar
military school, school where students learn to fight in wars
terra-cotta, baked red clay

◀ People placed these clay figures in the graves of children to keep them company in the afterlife.

BEFORE YOU GO ON . . .

1 How were boys' and girls' lives different in ancient Greece?

2 What toys did children play with?

HOW ABOUT YOU?
• Did your family have any special ceremonies when you were born?

GROWING UP IN ANCIENT ROME

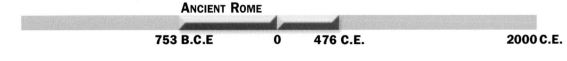

ANCIENT ROME			
753 B.C.E	0 476 C.E.		2000 C.E.

ANCIENT GREECE		
2000 B.C.E	323 B.C.E 0	2000 C.E.

When a Roman baby was born, a relative put the baby at the feet of the father. The father picked up the baby to accept it into the family. The baby was named nine days after birth.

The oldest man in a family—the father, the grandfather, or an uncle—was the "head of the family." However, women were also important to family life. They managed the house and household finances. In the early years of ancient Rome, women did not have many rights. In later years, they had more rights. They were allowed to own land and to have some types of jobs. They could manage some businesses. But they were still not allowed to hold jobs in the government or to become lawyers or teachers.

Girls and boys wore a special locket, called a *bulla*, around their necks. The bulla protected them from evil. A girl wore the bulla until her wedding day. A boy wore the bulla until he became a citizen. A boy became a citizen at age sixteen or seventeen. The family had a big celebration on this day.

In the third century, the Greeks **influenced** Roman education. Some Greeks lived in southern Italy. Greek teachers introduced the Romans to literature and philosophy.

▲ Roman children dressed like their parents. They wore long shirts called *tunics*.

◄ Marble heads of a Roman girl and boy ▼

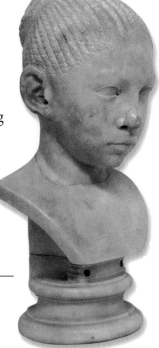

---

influenced, had an effect on; changed

▲ Glass and clay marbles

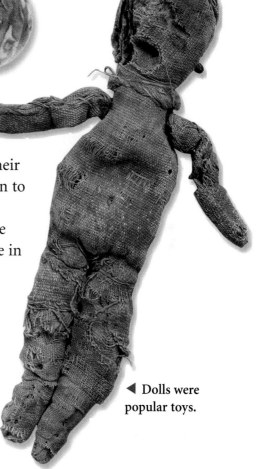

School was not free. Most children in ancient Rome were not from rich families. They were poor. In poor families, parents taught their children at home. Many poor children did not learn to read or write.

Rich families sent their children to school at age seven to learn basic subjects. Girls did not continue in school after they learned the basic subjects. They stayed at home, where their mothers taught them how to be good wives and mothers.

Boys from rich families continued their education in formal schools or with **tutors**. They became lawyers or worked in government.

What did children do after school? They played with friends, pets, or toys. Toys included balls, hobbyhorses, kites, **models** of people and animals, hoops, stilts, marbles, and knucklebones. War games were popular with boys. Girls played with dolls. They also played board games, tic-tac-toe, and ball games.

What kind of pets did children play with in ancient Rome? Dogs were the **favorite** pets. Other pets were birds, such as pigeons, ducks, quail, and geese. Some children even had monkeys.

◀ Dolls were popular toys.

---

tutors, teachers of one student or a small group of students
models, small copies
favorite, preferred over all others; best loved

BEFORE YOU GO ON . . .

1 What did girls do when they grew up?
2 What kind of work did boys from rich families do?

HOW ABOUT YOU?
• What do you do after school?

GROWING UP IN THE ANCIENT MAYA CULTURE

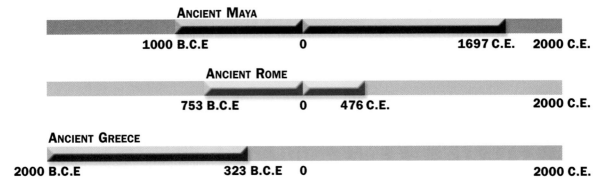

ANCIENT MAYA			
1000 B.C.E	0	1697 C.E.	2000 C.E.

ANCIENT ROME		
753 B.C.E	0	476 C.E.	2000 C.E.

ANCIENT GREECE		
2000 B.C.E	323 B.C.E	0	2000 C.E.

The Maya people lived in a large area of southern Mexico and Guatemala. They lived in enormous cities and created extraordinary art and **architecture**. You can visit the **ruins** of some ancient Maya cities, such as Chichén Itzá in Mexico.

The father was the head of the family. Maya men worked hard to support their families, and they paid **taxes** to the **government**. Women in Maya society cooked, made cloth and clothing, and took care of children.

When a boy was about five years old, the Maya tied a small white bead to the top of his head. When a girl was about five, the Maya tied a red shell around her waist. When boys and girls were twelve or thirteen years old, the village had a big ceremony that marked the end of childhood. During the ceremony, a priest cut the beads from the boys' heads. Mothers removed the red shells from the girls' waists. After the ceremony, boys and girls could get married. Young men painted themselves black until they were married.

▲ The Maya city of Chichén Itzá became a center for buying and selling goods.

All women did some weaving and spinning. They made things for their families and to sell. ▼

---

architecture, building design
ruins, the parts of buildings that are left after the rest have been destroyed
taxes, money paid to the government
government, people who rule a city or a country

◀ This Maya vase shows a jaguar.

▲ Dog on wheels

In Maya culture, school was free. Boys and girls learned from their parents, too. Girls learned how to weave and cook. Boys learned to hunt and fish. Children also learned how to grow food. At age seventeen, boys joined the army to learn about war and fighting.

Children played games and they played with toys. Some of their toys had wheels. Surprisingly, the Maya did not use wheels in their work or transportation. However, toys, such as animal pull-toys, had wheels.

Animals were important in everyday life and religion. The Maya used animals in their art. They decorated various items with pictures of foxes, owls, jaguars, hummingbirds, eagles, and other animals. The Maya ate some dogs. But they used most dogs for hunting. The Maya thought that dogs could **guide** people on the journey to the afterlife. They buried dogs with their owners.

___

guide, show the way

BEFORE YOU GO ON . . .

1. In which modern-day countries did the ancient Maya live?

2. Why did boys and girls have a special ceremony when they turned twelve or thirteen?

HOW ABOUT YOU?

- Can you cook? If so, what can you cook?

Review and Practice

Reread pages 6–7 of "Ancient Kids." Copy the Venn diagram into your notebook. Fill in more information for Greek boys (on the left side), Greek girls (on the right side), and both Greek boys and girls (in the center). Then compare diagrams in pairs.

Greek Boys

Started school at age 7

Learned reading, writing, mathematics

Helped in field

Learned to sail and fish

Greek Boys and Girls

Played with pets

Greek Girls

Learned to read and write at home

Helped mothers at home and with farming

A popular game was knucklebones. These were made from the ankle joints of small animals. ▶

12

EXTENSION

Copy the chart into your notebook. In the left column, write kids' activities in ancient Greece, ancient Rome, or the ancient Maya culture. In the right column, write *same* if you do the activity and *different* if you don't. Explain.

Ancient Kids	Me
Maya boys learned to hunt.	Different. I don't hunt.
Roman kids played with pets.	Same. I have a cat.

DISCUSSION

Discuss in pairs or small groups.

1. What are some examples of ceremonies in "Ancient Kids"? What ceremonies are important today?

2. How was a girl's life different from a boy's life in each of these cultures? How are the lives of boys and girls different today?

3. What did you do to preview the text? Did previewing help you understand the text? Explain.

4. Would you prefer to live in ancient Greece, ancient Rome, or the ancient Maya culture? Why?

Fables and Myths

Fables and myths are fiction. That means they are stories about imaginary people (or animals) and events. Most fables and myths are part of the "oral tradition"—they are told by parents to children. Their purpose is to entertain and instruct. Often fables have a "moral," or lesson, at the end.

Aesop's The Hare and the Tortoise

On a hot, sunny day, Hare saw Tortoise **plodding** along on the road. Hare **teased** Tortoise because she was walking so slowly.

Tortoise laughed. "You can tease me if you like, but I bet I can get to the end of the field before you can. Do you want to race?"

Hare agreed, thinking that he could easily win. He ran off. Tortoise plodded **steadily** after him.

Before long, Hare began to feel hot and tired. "I'll take a short **nap**," he thought. "If Tortoise passes me, I can **catch up to** her." Hare lay down and fell asleep.

Tortoise plodded on steadily, one foot after another.

The day was hot. Hare slept and slept in the heat. He slept for a longer time than he wanted. And Tortoise plodded on, slowly and steadily.

---

plodding, walking slowly
teased, made fun of; laughed at
steadily, at the same speed
nap, a short sleep
catch up to, go faster and pass

Finally, Hare woke up. He had slept longer than he wanted, but he still felt **confident** that he could reach the **finish line** before Tortoise.

He looked around. Tortoise was nowhere in sight. "Ha! Tortoise isn't even here yet!" he thought.

Hare started to run again. He leaped easily over roots and rocks. As he ran around the last corner and stopped to rest, he was amazed to see Tortoise, still plodding steadily on, one foot after another, nearer and nearer the finish line.

Now Hare ran as fast as he could. He almost flew! But it was too late. He threw himself over the finish line, but Tortoise was there first.

"So what do you say?" asked Tortoise. But Hare was too tired to answer.

MORAL: Slow and steady wins the race.

LITERARY ELEMENT

Personification is giving human traits to animals or things. Can you find personification in "The Hare and the Tortoise"?

---

confident, sure; certain
finish line, end of the race

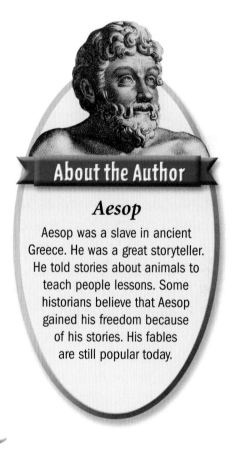

About the Author

Aesop

Aesop was a slave in ancient Greece. He was a great storyteller. He told stories about animals to teach people lessons. Some historians believe that Aesop gained his freedom because of his stories. His fables are still popular today.

BEFORE YOU GO ON . . .

1 Who are the two characters in this story?

2 Why does Hare decide to take a nap?

HOW ABOUT YOU?
- Who did you want to win the race? Why?

15

This is a myth of the Native American Pima tribe in Arizona. Like a fable, a myth is a short fictional story. Myths explain something about nature or the world.

Why Rattlesnake Has Fangs

Cheryl Giff

Rattlesnake used to be the gentlest little animal. The Sun God forgot to give Rattlesnake a **weapon** to protect himself, and he was called the Soft Child.

The animals liked to hear him rattle, so they teased him all the time. One day at a ceremonial dance, a mean little rabbit said, "Let's have some fun with Soft Child."

He started to throw helpless little Rattlesnake around.

"Catch," yelled Skunk as he threw Soft Child back to Rabbit.

They had a good time, but Rattlesnake was unhappy and there was nothing he could do about it.

The Sun God felt sorry for the sad little snake, and he told him what to do.

"Get two sharp **thorns** from the devil's claw plant and put them in your mouth."

---

fangs, big, sharp teeth
weapon, something you use to fight with
thorns, sharp spikes on a plant

Rattlesnake picked the devil's claw and put the thorns in his upper jaw.

"Now you will have to rattle to give a **warning**," the Sun God told him. "**Strike** only if you have to."

The next day, Rabbit started to kick the snake and throw him around the way he always did.

Rattlesnake began to rattle his warning, but Rabbit just laughed and kicked him again. Soft Child remembered the thorns he held in his mouth. He used them on Rabbit.

After that, every animal backed away from Rattlesnake, and he was not called Soft Child any longer.

To this day, Rattlesnake strikes only if he has to, but everyone fears him.

---

warning, sign that something bad will happen
strike, hit

BEFORE YOU GO ON . . .

1 How does the Sun God help Rattlesnake?

2 What does this myth explain?

HOW ABOUT YOU?
- Are you afraid of snakes? Explain.

Link the Readings

Think about "Ancient Kids," and reread the fable and the myth. Then copy the chart into your notebook and complete it.

Title of Selection	Type of Text (Genre)	Fiction or Nonfiction	Purpose of Selection	Culture
"Ancient Kids"	informational text	nonfiction	to inform	Greek, Roman, Maya
"The Hare and the Tortoise"	fable	fiction	to instruct and entertain	
"Why Rattlesnake Has Fangs"	myth		to instruct and entertain	

DISCUSSION

Discuss in pairs or small groups.

1. List the animals from the readings in your notebook. Which is your favorite? Which don't you like? Why?

2. Take turns telling a fable or myth. Use your own words. You can use "The Hare and the Tortoise," "Why Rattlesnake Has Fangs," or another fable or myth.

3. With your partner, discuss how you previewed "The Hare and the Tortoise" and "Why Rattlesnake Has Fangs." Did previewing help you understand the stories? How?

Connect to Writing

GRAMMAR

Using Adjectives to Describe

Use **adjectives** to describe nouns (people, places, and things).

Adjectives can come after the verb *be*.

> *be* adjective
> The tortoise is **slow**.

Adjectives can also come before the noun.

> *be* adjective noun
> The tortoise is a **slow animal**.
>
> *have* adjective noun
> The tortoise has **short legs**.

Do not add *-s* to adjectives when they describe more than one noun.

> Tortoises have short legs.
> NOT Tortoises have short~~s~~ legs.

Practice

Use the words to make sentences in your notebook. Pay attention to correct use and position of adjectives.

Examples: a big / is / Rome / city   Rome is a big city.
hair / Maria / has / black   Maria has black hair.
fast / are / hares / animals   Hares are fast animals.

1. blue / John / eyes / has
2. Rome and Athens / cities / ancient / are
3. a fast animal / is / not / Tortoise
4. pets / good / Dogs and cats / are
5. have / Rattlesnakes / fangs / sharp

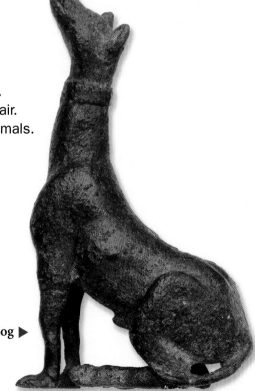

A Roman guard dog ▶

18

SKILLS FOR WRITING

Writing Correct Sentences

Remember these rules when you write sentences.

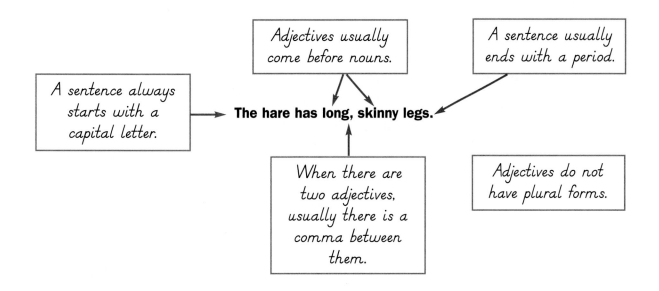

Adjectives usually come before nouns.

A sentence usually ends with a period.

A sentence always starts with a capital letter.

The hare has long, skinny legs.

When there are two adjectives, usually there is a comma between them.

Adjectives do not have plural forms.

Practice

Correct these sentences in your notebook. Use the rules above.

1. girls didn't leave their houses very often
2. tortoise met hare on a day hot
3. hare was a nasty mean animal
4. they learned how to be citizens goods
5. boys from families rich had tutors

WRITING ASSIGNMENT

Descriptive Sentences

You will write six sentences to describe a family member, a friend, or yourself.

1. Read Look for adjectives in the stories on pages 14–16. In your notebook, list adjectives that describe each character.

Writing Strategy: Word Web

A word web helps you prepare to write a description. It helps you plan before you write. Look at the word web about Juan.

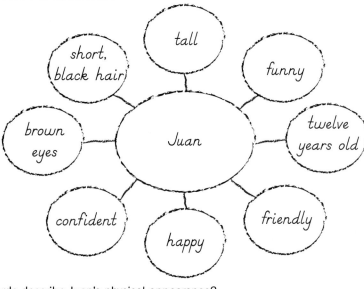

1. What words describe Juan's physical appearance?
2. What words describe Juan's personality?

2. Make a word web Draw a word web in your notebook. Write the name of the person you are describing in the center circle. Write adjectives that describe the person in circles around it.

3. Write Use your word web to write six sentences about the person. Remember the rules for writing correct sentences.

EDITING CHECKLIST

Did you . . .

► start each sentence with a capital letter?

► end each sentence with a period?

► put adjectives in the correct place?

20

Check Your Knowledge

Language Development

1. What is one way to find the meaning of a new word?

2. Describe previewing a text. How does previewing help you understand the text?

3. What is the purpose of informational texts? Of fables? Of myths?

4. What is personification? Give an example.

5. How can a word web help you write?

6. What are adjectives? Give three examples. Where do they usually come in a sentence?

7. What do the timelines in "Ancient Kids" tell you?

Academic Content

1. What new social studies vocabulary did you learn in Part 1? What do the words mean?

2. What three cultures did you read about in "Ancient Kids"?

3. How is your life different from the life of a girl or boy in the ancient Maya culture?

4. Who was Aesop?

Prepare to Read

OBJECTIVES

LANGUAGE DEVELOPMENT

Reading:
- Vocabulary building: *Context, dictionary skills*
- Reading strategy: *Predicting*
- Text types: *Novel, science article*
- Literary element: *Point of view*

Writing:
- Descriptive writing
- Graphic organizers: *Word web, charts*
- Editing checklist

Listening/Speaking:
- Appreciation: *Story, article*
- Discussing ideas
- Compare and contrast

Grammar:
- Conjunction *and*
- Compound sentences

Viewing/Representing:
- Illustrations, charts, diagrams, photographs

ACADEMIC CONTENT
- Science vocabulary
- Growth in plants and animals
- Measurements

BACKGROUND

Later, Gator is a novel. A novel is fiction. Novels are usually longer than fables or myths. *Later, Gator* is about a boy who gives his little brother a very unusual present. You will read an excerpt—or small part—of this novel.

Make connections Think of presents people have given you. Then copy the chart into your notebook and complete it. Share your chart with a partner.

Present	When did you get it?	Who gave it to you?	Did you like it?

LEARN KEY WORDS

birthday presents
get along with
imagination
normal
reptiles
special

VOCABULARY

Read these sentences. Use the context to figure out the meaning of the **red** words. Use a dictionary to check your answers. Write each word and its meaning in your notebook.

1. When he turned twelve years old, he got lots of **birthday presents**—toys, books, and clothes.
2. They **get along with** each other very well. They never fight.
3. When you write fiction, you have to use your **imagination**.
4. It is **normal** to feel tired after running a long way.
5. I hate **reptiles**, especially snakes and lizards.
6. His birthday is a **special** day. He eats cake and gets presents.

READING STRATEGY

Predicting

You will understand a text better if you **predict**, or guess what will happen next, as you read. Follow these steps:

- stop sometimes and ask yourself, "What will happen next?"
- look for clues in the story and illustrations
- think about what you already know
- think about your own experiences

Then continue reading to see if your prediction is correct.

what you know so far → predictions

clues from text → your own experiences → predictions

Preview the text. As you read, try to find clues in the text and illustrations that help you predict what will happen next.

from Later, Gator

Laurence Yep

In this story, Teddy, the narrator, is jealous of his younger brother, Bobby, because everyone likes him. When their mother asks Teddy to buy Bobby a birthday present, Teddy plans to buy him something that he hopes will scare Bobby.

The alligator was Mother's fault. She told me to buy something special. Mother, as usual, **blames** me. She says that I've got more imagination than brains.

That's not my little brother's problem. Last Christmas I gave him a pair of socks. Bobby was too dumb to understand the insult. Instead of getting mad, he said to me, "They're **neat-o** and just what I wanted."

Yeah, sure, I thought to myself.

Bobby had to put on his new socks right away and wriggle his toes at me. "They're very warm and comfortable. Thank you," he said.

Do you see what I mean? Bobby is a walking Hallmark card.

---

blames, says someone did something bad
neat-o, great (slang)

24

A *narrator* tells a story from his or her *point of view.*
- In first-person point of view, the narrator tells his or her own story using *I* and *my.*
- In third-person point of view, the narrator tells someone else's story using *he* or *she.*

Mother had understood, though. So this year, on Friday, the week before Bobby's eighth birthday, she took me aside. "Why can't you get along with your little brother? What has he ever done to you?"

"Nothing," I confessed. That was the trouble. What kind of little brother doesn't **bug** his big brother? Bobby was not normal.

Mother clicked her tongue. "Everybody else likes your brother. He's so sweet."

"Bobby's a regular mint chocolate bar, all right," I said, and thought to myself, And I am a raisin cookie.

"Then why haven't you ever bought him something special?" Mother demanded. She would make a good **prosecutor**.

"You always said it's the **spirit** that counts," I grumbled.

Mother frowned. "Only a mean person buys a cheap pair of white cotton socks."

"He liked the baseball."

Mother folded her hands in front of her. "Which you then used and lost."

"The Christmas before I got him comic books," I pointed out.

"Which he couldn't read."

"I read them to him," I said. Mother just looked at me until I admitted, "Sometimes."

"You treat him like he's an enemy. Don't you love your brother?" Mother asked.

"Of course I do," I lied. (But really, how can I love a little angel who makes me feel mean and selfish and bad?)

"Then show your love," Mother said. "Get something Bobby wants."

I tried to **weasel out of** it. "I can't afford the official **Willie Mays** baseball glove."

"No, I mean something he wants even more. I've talked it over with your father, and he's agreed that Bobby is now old enough to have a pet," Mother said.

She went to a cabinet and took out a big paper bag. From the bag, she slid out a kidney-shaped plastic tray. A wall of transparent plastic some three inches high ran around the edge of the tray. Part of the bottom rose up into an **island** in the center. A plastic palm tree grew from the island's middle.

---

bug, annoy; bother
prosecutor, lawyer who asks questions in court
spirit, thought or attitude

weasel out of, avoid
Willie Mays, famous baseball player
island, land surrounded by water

BEFORE YOU GO ON . . .

1 What does Mother want Teddy to do?

2 Who is the narrator of the story?

HOW ABOUT YOU?
- Do you have a younger brother or sister? If so, describe him or her.

"I got the idea when he was watching a nature show on TV. He likes animals," Mother said. "He always wants to go to the zoo or the Academy of Sciences." The academy was in Golden Gate Park and had an aquarium, a hall with stuffed animals, and a reptile section.

It wasn't fair, I told myself. I figured he watched educational shows to please our parents and to make me look bad. I'll take the **Three Stooges** over a nature show anytime.

"Then I saw an ad in the newspaper," Mother said, "and I bought this. It's a turtle home. You go down to the department store. They've got turtles on sale. You can buy him a pet."

Feeling **miserable** but caught, I promised.

For the rest of the week, I put it off. There was no fun in giving Bobby something he wanted. Instead, I just hung around the apartment and **moped**.

On the morning of his birthday, he was up bright and early and jumping around, pretending to catch fly balls over the shoulder like Willie Mays. He had made so much noise that I had got up early, too, even though it was Saturday.

Mother served his favorite breakfast. We each had a scrambled egg with rice and slices of Chinese sausage. The problem was that Mother served it every morning. It was typical of Bobby to play up to Mother that way. I would have asked for scrambled eggs, bacon, and toast.

When Father asked Bobby what he wanted to do on his birthday, Bobby **volunteered** to help him in the fish shop. Any normal kid would have asked for money for a movie—for him and for his older brother. Boy, he really **drove me crazy**.

After Father and Bobby left for work, Mother stood over me. "Well, did you buy Bobby's pet?" she asked.

I **squirmed** on my chair. "I didn't want to get it too soon. If Bobby found it, it would ruin the surprise."

"I thought so." Mother handed me a folded-up piece of paper. "I cut out the ad from the newspaper so you would know where to go. After you wash the dishes, go down and buy Bobby's pet."

"That's Bobby's chore today," I whined.

"It's his birthday," Mother said. "I have to buy tonight's dinner. When I come home, I want to find that turtle waiting for me. You can leave it in our bedroom until we give out the presents." She wasn't going to leave me any way to **escape**. "If you need money, go down to the garbage cans. I saw lots of empty soda bottles."

---

volunteered, offered to do something
drove me crazy, made me angry
squirmed, turned and twisted
escape, get away from something

BEFORE YOU GO ON . . .

1 Why does Mother think Bobby likes animals?

2 Why doesn't Teddy want to buy Bobby a turtle?

HOW ABOUT YOU?
- What do you like to do on your birthday?

Three Stooges, popular TV comedians
miserable, very unhappy
moped, felt sad

After Mother left, I heaved a big sigh. Going into the kitchen, I turned on the radio for music and began washing the dishes.

As I was finishing up, I saw the newspaper ad on the table. It was for a department store in the Stonestown mall, where Mother worked. It would take me most of the morning to get out there.

Above the address was a big drawing of a boy and girl **gazing** happily at a turtle. It was grinning back from a plastic bowl like the one Mother had bought. In big type, the ad announced the turtles were on sale for fifty cents. Then I saw the small print: BABY ALLIGATORS ON SALE. And like an **omen**, the radio began playing a funny song from the past. "See you later, alligator," the radio sang. "After a while, crocodile."

If there had been a light bulb over my head, it would have suddenly shone as bright as the sun. Carefully I reviewed Mother's words. As far as I could remember, she had said to buy Bobby a pet. I chuckled. Poor Mother. She thought she had trapped me, but she had given me a **loophole**.

---

gazing, staring

omen, sign that something will happen
loophole, something that lets you escape

A plan began to build in my mind. First, though, I called up the department store having the sale. When I got the **operator**, I asked her, "I'd like to buy my brother something special from your pet department. If he doesn't like it, can I return it?"

"You can return anything within seventy-two hours after the sale." She added, "But the pet has to be alive."

"It won't be here long enough to die," I laughed, and hung up. I imagined what would happen tonight when Bobby opened his present. He would probably run **shrieking** from the room.

In my mind, I played out many **marvelous** scenes, ranging from a **horrified** Bobby to an **outraged** one. In any case, I would have to return it and get my money back. At the same time Mother would learn her lesson too.

It was the perfect gift. I could keep my promise to Mother because it would be nature stuff as well as something special. I could keep my promise to myself because it would be weird enough.

---

operator, someone who answers phone calls
shrieking, screaming
marvelous, good; wonderful
horrified, very upset
outraged, extremely angry

About the Author

Laurence Yep

Laurence Yep is a Chinese-American writer. He writes stories for children and adults. He was born in 1948, in California. When he was young, Yep really did buy his little brother an alligator as a pet!

BEFORE YOU GO ON . . .

1. What does Teddy think Bobby will do when he opens the present?
2. Does Teddy have a good imagination? Explain.

HOW ABOUT YOU?
- Would you like to get an alligator as a birthday present? Why or why not?

Review and Practice

Reread the excerpt from *Later, Gator.* Number the events in chronological (time) order. Remember, the story includes events that took place before Mother asks Teddy to buy a special present for his brother. Write the sentences in your notebook.

_____ Bobby eats his birthday breakfast.

_____ Teddy's mother asks him to buy Bobby a pet.

___1___ Teddy gives Bobby a pair of white socks for Christmas.

_____ Teddy does the dishes because it's Bobby's birthday.

_____ Teddy calls the department store.

_____ Mother gives Teddy a newspaper ad with directions on it.

_____ Teddy has an idea that makes him happy.

_____ Bobby volunteers to help in the fish shop.

EXTENSION

1. Look at the words in the box. Do you know what they mean? If not, look them up in your dictionary.

friendly	**jealous**	**funny**	**selfish**
helpful	**thankful**	**kind**	**mean**

Copy these word webs into your notebook. Write adjectives that describe the boys in the empty circles. Use words from the box. Then compare word webs in small groups.

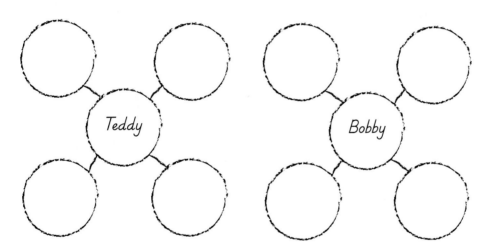

2. Compare yourself to Bobby and Teddy.

DISCUSSION

Discuss in pairs or small groups.

1. Is an alligator a good pet? Why or why not?
2. What predictions did you make as you read the story? Were your predictions correct? What were some clues you used to make predictions? How do you predict *Later, Gator* will end?

This is an informational text. It gives some facts about growth. Look at the title, headings, and pictures. What do you think the text is about?

AMAZING GROWTH FACTS

It is one of the wonders of nature that all living things **increase** in size. Think about how a tiny acorn can grow into an enormous oak tree. Sometimes this growth is very fast, other times it is very slow.

The **average** newborn baby is 50 centimeters long and weighs 3.4 kilograms. When the baby grows up, he or she increases to three times that **length** and 18 times that **weight**. Girls and boys are about the same **height** and weight until early adulthood. Then boys usually grow taller and weigh more than girls.

Bamboo can grow 90 centimeters in one day—the height of an average three-year-old child.

Pacific giant kelp (a kind of seaweed) can grow as much as 45 centimeters in one day.

An ant can lift more than 100 times its weight. One hundred times the weight of a 64-kilogram person would be the same weight as three cars!

▲ If we were as strong as ants, we could lift three cars!

— Bamboo: 30 m

Pacific giant kelp: 60 m —

Average man: 1.75 m

---

increase, become bigger
average, usual or normal
length, how long something is
weight, how heavy something is
height, how tall something is

A baby kangaroo is the size and weight of a paper clip (1 gram). An adult kangaroo is 30,000 times heavier (30 kilograms). If a human grew at this rate, a 3.4-kilogram baby would weigh 102,000 kilograms as an adult—that's as much as a large whale! An average man weighs about 80 kilograms.

The egg of a golden eagle and the egg of a Nile crocodile are both 8 centimeters long. But look how much bigger the crocodile grows!

A 26-centimeter baby crocodile can grow into a 5-meter adult crocodile. If humans grew at the same **rate** as Nile crocodiles, a 50-centimeter baby would grow into a 9.5-meter adult—more than 5 times as tall as the average person!

---

rate, speed

Paperclip

Joey:
1 g

Adult kangaroo:
30 kg

BEFORE YOU GO ON . . .

1 Using the Conversion Chart, convert the metric measurements in the text to imperial measurements.

2 Which grows fastest in one day—humans, bamboo, or Pacific giant kelp? Which grows biggest—eagles, crocodiles, or humans?

HOW ABOUT YOU?
• What growth fact do you find most interesting?

Conversion Chart

metric	imperial
1 millimeter	= 0.039 inches
1 centimeter	= 0.39 inches
1 meter	= 3.28 feet
1 gram	= 0.035 ounces
1 kilogram	= 2.2 pounds

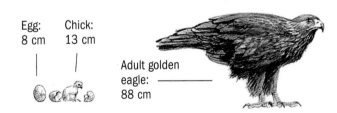

Egg:
8 cm

Chick:
13 cm

Adult golden eagle:
88 cm

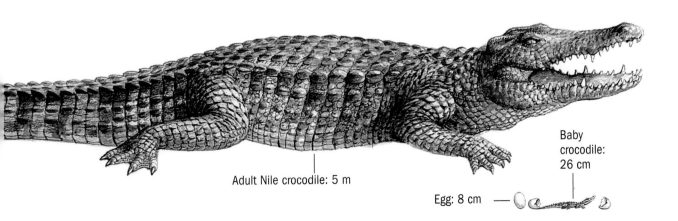

Adult Nile crocodile: 5 m

Baby crocodile:
26 cm

Egg: 8 cm

33

Clams are among the longest living and slowest growing of all **creatures**. A deep-sea clam takes 100 years to grow 8 millimeters. That's as big as your fingernail!

Do you ever wonder where the dust in your home comes from? Much of it **is made up of** the 50,000 or so microscopic **flakes** of skin that fall off of you every minute. All the skin **shed** by a person in a 70-year lifetime weighs almost as much as the average 6-year-old child (20 kilograms).

In the average human life of 70 years, a heart pumps enough blood around the body to fill the fuel tanks of 700 **jumbo jets**. The food that we eat in our lifetime is equal in weight to the weight of 6 elephants! A horse's **intestines** are about 27 meters long. A human's intestines are about 7.5 meters long. Luckily, the intestines are curled up inside the body. Otherwise, people and horses would look very strange!

▲ Slow-growing clam

▲ A lifetime of shed skin

---

creatures, animals or insects
is made up of, consists of; contains
flakes, small, thin pieces
shed, lost by
jumbo jets, very big airplanes
intestines, tubes that take food from your stomach out of your body

BEFORE YOU GO ON . . .

1 What is dust mostly made up of?

2 How long are the intestines of humans? Of horses?

HOW ABOUT YOU?

- How tall are you in meters and in feet? How much have you grown in the past year?

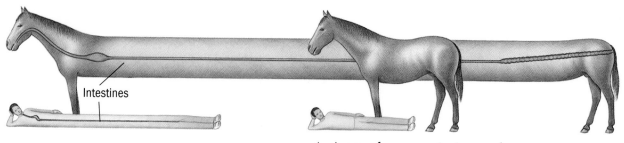

Intestines

▲ Average human   ▲ Average horse

Link the Readings

REFLECTION

Reread "Amazing Growth Facts." Think about the two texts you read as you look at the chart. Then copy the chart into your notebook and complete it. Discuss your information with a partner.

Title of Selection	Type of Text (Genre)	Fiction or Nonfiction	Purpose of Selection	What I Liked About It
From *Later, Gator*	*novel*		*to entertain*	
"Amazing Growth Facts"	*informational text*	*nonfiction*	*to inform*	

DISCUSSION

Discuss in pairs or small groups.

1. Alligators grow to about 5 meters (13 ft.) long and live for about eighty years. Do you think that Teddy's idea to give Bobby an alligator as a pet was a good one? Why or why not?

2. Which reading did you find more interesting—the excerpt from *Later, Gator* or "Amazing Growth Facts"? Why?

Giant sequoia: 84 m ▶

Giraffe: 5.8 m ▶

Human: 1.6 m ▲

35

Connect to Writing

GRAMMAR

Using the Conjunction *and*

A **conjunction** connects words, groups of words, and sentences. Use *and* to connect words in a sentence.

> The socks were warm **and** comfortable.
>
> Bobby makes Teddy feel mean **and** selfish.
>
> Teddy bought socks **and** books.

Use *and* to connect groups of words in a sentence.

> Bobby likes to play ball **and** to watch nature shows.
>
> Teddy read the ad **and** called the store.

Use *and* to connect sentences. When *and* is used to connect two sentences, you usually put a comma before it.

> Bobby got up early, **and** he ate breakfast.
>
> Teddy went to the store, **and** he bought a present.

Practice

Copy the sentences into your notebook. Circle the conjunction *and.* Then underline the words, groups of words, or sentences that the conjunction connects.

Example: Teddy <u>used</u> (and) <u>lost</u> Bobby's baseball.

1. Bobby likes eggs and rice.
2. Mother got an ad and gave it to Teddy.
3. Teddy listened to his mother, and he bought a pet for Bobby.
4. Teddy had a plan, and it was a big surprise.
5. Teddy washed the dishes and bought a present.
6. Teddy was older and smarter.
7. Teddy turned on the radio, and he heard a funny song.

SKILLS FOR WRITING

Writing Compound Sentences

When you combine two simple sentences by using *and*, change the period of the first sentence to a comma and change the first letter of the second sentence into a lowercase letter. The new sentence is called a **compound sentence**. It is made up of two simple sentences.

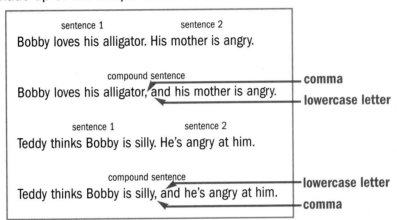

```
           sentence 1           sentence 2
     Bobby loves his alligator. His mother is angry.

              compound sentence                         ─── comma
     Bobby loves his alligator, and his mother is angry.
                                                        ─── lowercase letter

           sentence 1           sentence 2
     Teddy thinks Bobby is silly. He's angry at him.

              compound sentence                         ─── lowercase letter
     Teddy thinks Bobby is silly, and he's angry at him.
                                                        ─── comma
```

Practice

Read the sentences. Combine them to make compound sentences. Write them in your notebook.

Example: Teddy likes eggs and bacon. Bobby does too.
Teddy likes eggs and bacon, and Bobby does too.

1. Bamboo grows quickly. Clams grow slowly.

2. Some growth facts are strange. Some are funny.

3. Bobby likes alligators. His mother likes turtles.

4. Teddy gets angry at Bobby. Bobby smiles at Teddy.

5. Bobby liked the socks. He likes the books too.

WRITING TIPS

- A sentence always begins with a capital letter.
- A sentence usually ends with a period.

WRITING ASSIGNMENT

Descriptive Sentences

You will write three compound sentences to describe a family member, a friend, or another person you know.

1. **Read** Reread the compound sentences on page 37. What word is used to combine the sentences? What punctuation mark is used between the two parts of the sentences?

Writing Strategy: Sentence-Combining Chart

A sentence-combining chart will help you join two simple sentences. Read the sentences. Then look at the chart.

Bobby is happy. Everyone loves him.
Teddy is mean. His mother is angry at him.

Simple Sentence	,	and	Simple Sentence
Bobby is happy	,	and	everyone loves him.
Teddy is mean	,	and	his mother is angry at him.

1. What conjunction joins the two sentences?
2. What punctuation mark separates the two parts of the sentence?

2. **Make a sentence-combining chart** Draw a sentence-combining chart in your notebook.

3. **Write** Write six simple sentences describing a family member, a friend, or another person you know. Then use your six simple sentences and your sentence-combining chart to make three compound sentences. Check your sentences in pairs.

Check Your Knowledge

Language Development

1. How can you check word definitions when you use context to figure out their meanings?

2. How can you use predicting as a reading strategy? Give an example.

3. In *Later, Gator,* what do you predict will happen when Bobby opens his present from Teddy?

4. What is a novel? How is it similar to a fable or myth? How is it different from a fable or myth?

5. What is point of view? From whose point of view is *Later, Gator* told?

6. What is a conjunction? Give an example of a compound sentence that you make using a conjunction.

7. Do the illustrations in "Amazing Growth Facts" help you understand the comparisons? Why or why not?

Academic Content

1. What new science vocabulary did you learn in Part 2? What do the words mean?

2. Do humans, animals, and plants grow at the same rate? Give some examples.

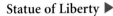

Statue of Liberty ▶

▲ Sequoia

Put It All Together

OBJECTIVES

Integrate Skills
- **Listening/ Speaking:** *Group presentation*
- **Writing:** *Descriptive paragraph*

Investigate Themes
- **Projects**
- **Further reading**

LISTENING and SPEAKING WORKSHOP

GROUP PRESENTATION

You will organize and give a group presentation about important qualities in a friend.

1 **Think about it** Ask yourself these questions: What qualities do I want in a friend? What kind of personality does she or he have? List five adjectives that describe a good friend.

Work in groups of four. Use your list of adjectives to brainstorm a longer list of all the qualities that your group thinks are important.

2 **Organize** Choose one group member to make the presentation to the class. Work together to create a description of an "ideal friend." Make some notes to help the speaker organize what he or she is going to say.

3 **Practice** Listen to your group speaker present. Ask questions and make comments.

4 **Present and evaluate** Present your group's description to the class. After each group finishes, evaluate the presentation. What did you like best about the description? Do you have suggestions for improvement?

SPEAKING TIPS

- Make eye contact with as many people as you can.
- Speak clearly and loudly enough for everyone to hear.

LISTENING TIP

If you don't understand something a speaker says, you can say,

- "I don't understand. Can you explain, please?"
- "Could you repeat that, please?"

WRITING WORKSHOP

DESCRIPTIVE PARAGRAPH

In descriptive writing, the writer uses adjectives to help the reader picture or imagine what a person (or place or thing) is like. Some adjectives describe people's physical characteristics, or what they look like—for example, *short, tall, thin*. Other adjectives describe people's personal qualities or characteristics, such as *friendly, happy, loyal*. In a descriptive paragraph, a writer may also describe a person's abilities or skills.

A good descriptive paragraph includes the following characteristics:

- an interesting introductory sentence to get your readers' attention
- adjectives that help the reader picture or imagine the person
- details or examples that describe the person's abilities or skills

You will write a paragraph describing a person. You can write about a family member, friend, or someone you know. Use the following steps and the model on page 42 to help you.

1 **Prewrite** Make a list of family members, friends, or other people you know. Choose one person to write about. Think about the person you want to describe. What does he or she look like? What special qualities or characteristics does he or she have? Make a word web to organize your ideas.

WRITING TIP

A **paragraph** is a group of sentences about one idea in a piece of writing. The introductory sentence is the first sentence of the paragraph. An interesting introductory sentence makes your reader want to read more.

41

Before you write a first draft of your descriptive paragraph, read the model.
Notice the characteristics of a descriptive paragraph.

Will Trigg

My Friend Greg

My friend Greg is an (easy-going), (loyal,) and (funny) guy. He never gets angry, and he can always make me laugh. Greg is (tall) and (thin,) and he has (black) hair and (brown) eyes. He is very (athletic,) and he likes soccer and horseback riding. Dogs are his favorite animals, but he likes cats, too. Unfortunately, Greg moved to Massachusetts this year, so now we can't see each other very often. I wish we could live next door to each other. If that wish comes true, I will be very happy.

The writer begins with an interesting introductory sentence.

He uses adjectives to describe his friend's physical and personal characteristics.

He describes what his friend likes

He describes his feelings for his friend.

42

2 **Draft** Use the model and your word web to write your descriptive paragraph.

- Start your paragraph with an interesting introductory sentence, so your reader will want to read your description. Notice how the student starts his paragraph. How does he get you interested in reading about his friend?

- Use adjectives to describe the person's physical and personal characteristics, so your reader can imagine what he or she is like.

- Include details or examples of his or her abilities and interests.

3 **Edit** Work in pairs. Trade papers and read each other's paragraphs. Use the questions in the editing checklist to evaluate each other's work.

EDITING CHECKLIST

Did you . . .

- ▶ write an interesting introductory sentence?
- ▶ use adjectives to describe the person?
- ▶ use *and* correctly?
- ▶ capitalize the first letter of words in the title?
- ▶ begin each sentence with a capital letter?
- ▶ end each sentence with a period?

4 **Revise** Revise your paragraph. Add information and correct mistakes if necessary.

5 **Publish** Share your paragraph with your teacher and classmates.

PROJECTS

Work in pairs or small groups. Choose one of these projects.

1 Talk to older family members or friends about their childhood. What do they remember about growing up? What did they wear? What games did they like to play? What did they do after school? Make a timeline about their life.

2 Reread "Why Rattlesnake Has Fangs." Think of another animal with a special body part, like a monkey (tail) or a butterfly (wings). Write a story about how that animal got its special body part. Draw pictures to go with your story.

3 Go to the library and find a book of fables. Choose one fable with two or three animal characters. With one or two friends, act out the fable for your classmates. Find a piece of music that goes along with your story. Play it in the background as you act out the story.

4 Collect more "amazing facts" about how plants and animals grow. Look in books, in magazines, and on the Internet. Include pictures.

5 Use the Internet to find out more about ancient cultures. Type in key words like *ancient Greece, ancient Rome*, or *ancient Maya*. Find out more about the daily lives of the people who lived in ancient times. Make a poster illustrating your research. Share your poster with your class.

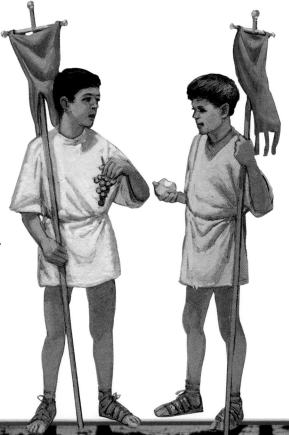

To find out more about the theme of this unit, choose from these reading suggestions.

Little Women, **Louisa May Alcott** This story is about the four March sisters—tomboy Jo, pretty Meg, ailing Beth, and headstrong Amy—as they develop from girls into young women. The sisters face the joys and sorrows of growing up.

Treasure Island, **Robert Louis Stevenson** Young Jim Hawkins lives quietly with his parents until a man named Billy Bones moves in. When Bones dies, Jim encounters Dr. Livesey and the Squire. The three discover a treasure map among Bones's belongings and decide to sail to the island where the treasure is buried. Jim's adventures help him grow into a brave, mature, confident young man.

Gladiator, **Dewey Gram** This story tells of a great general, Maximus, who served the Roman Empire in 180 C.E. Maximus is forced into exile and slavery after Emperor Marcus Aurelius dies and his scheming son, Commodus, takes the throne. Maximus becomes a champion gladiator and hero of the people.

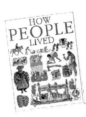

How People Lived, **Anne Millard** This book takes the reader through a typical day in the lives of people from prehistoric times through early civilizations to the Middle Ages and the Renaissance. It shows what people ate, what they used for shelter, and what they did at home and at work. The book also describes how archaeologists learn about ancient lifestyles.

Under the Royal Palms: A Childhood in Cuba, **Alma Flor Ada** The author recollects growing up in a small Cuban town and the many people who touched her life, including her grandmother with whom she counted bats, a mysterious uncle, and a dance teacher who helped her through a difficult year at school. Gentle, sad, and funny, this book is about the importance of family, friends, neighbors, and teachers to a young girl's life.

UNIT 2

Challenges and Choices

46

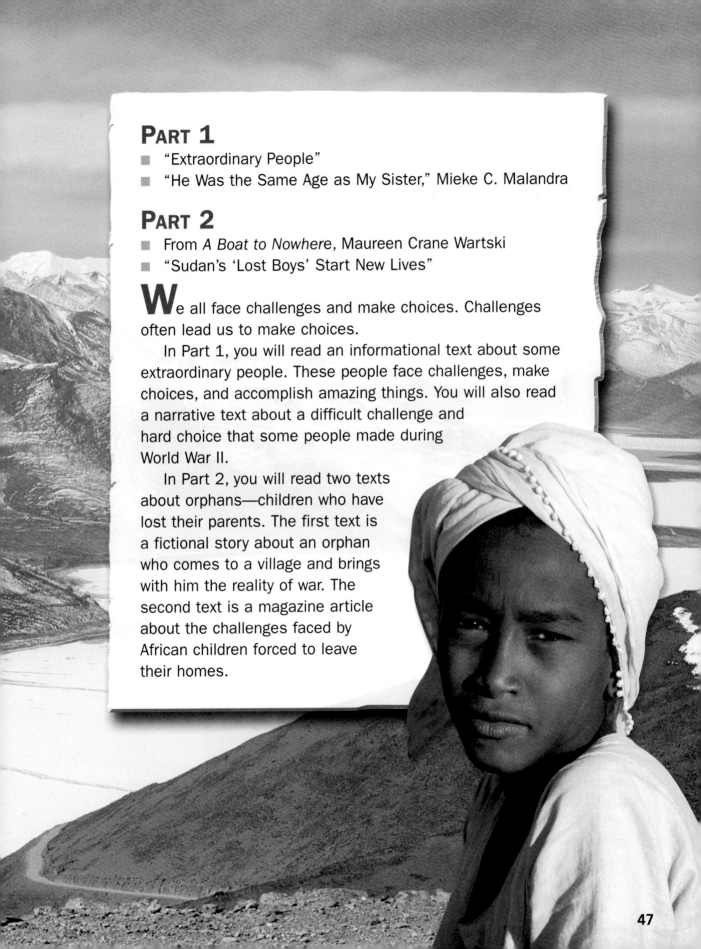

PART 1

■ "Extraordinary People"

■ "He Was the Same Age as My Sister," Mieke C. Malandra

PART 2

■ From *A Boat to Nowhere*, Maureen Crane Wartski

■ "Sudan's 'Lost Boys' Start New Lives"

We all face challenges and make choices. Challenges often lead us to make choices.

In Part 1, you will read an informational text about some extraordinary people. These people face challenges, make choices, and accomplish amazing things. You will also read a narrative text about a difficult challenge and hard choice that some people made during World War II.

In Part 2, you will read two texts about orphans—children who have lost their parents. The first text is a fictional story about an orphan who comes to a village and brings with him the reality of war. The second text is a magazine article about the challenges faced by African children forced to leave their homes.

Prepare to Read

BACKGROUND

"Extraordinary People" is an informational text. It gives biographical information about several important people from the past and the present. The text will tell you about the challenges and choices these extraordinary people made.

Make connections We all face challenges and make choices every day, in different ways. Look at these pictures and answer the questions.

1. What challenges are these people facing?
2. Have you ever faced any of these challenges?
3. How do you think these people feel about their challenges?
4. What challenges do you face in your life?

LEARN KEY WORDS

disability
extraordinary
incapable
uncommon
underachiever
unusual

VOCABULARY

Some words in English have prefixes. A prefix is a group of letters at the beginning of a word that changes its meaning and makes a new word. If you know the meaning of the prefix, it can help you understand the new word.

Prefix	Meaning	Word	New Word
dis-	opposite or negative	ability	disability
extra-	more than usual	ordinary	extraordinary
in-	opposite	capable	incapable
under-	less than usual	achiever	underachiever
un-	not	usual common	unusual uncommon

READING STRATEGY

Skimming a Text to Determine Major Ideas

Skimming a text is a strategy that good readers use when they read a new or difficult text. Skimming, like previewing, helps you to become more familiar with the text. It also helps you set your purpose for reading the text.

To skim a text:

- read it very quickly to get the main ideas only
- don't stop at words you don't know—skip over them

You'll be surprised at how much of a text you can understand when you skim. When you've finished skimming, you can go back for a more careful reading.

Social Studies

First, preview the text. Then skim it. Try to keep reading until you've finished the section on each person. Don't stop when you see a word you don't understand. The second time you read through the text, you can use the glosses and context clues to figure out the meanings of new words.

Extraordinary People

Rosa Parks (1913–) left work and **boarded** a bus in Montgomery, Alabama, on a December evening in 1955. In those days in Alabama, African Americans and white people were separated on buses. White people sat in the front of the bus, and African-American people sat in the back. On this particular evening, Parks sat in the front row of the "colored" section.

The bus became crowded, and the bus driver told Parks to give her seat to a white passenger. But she **refused**.

Parks was **arrested** by the police. But she was a well-known woman in the community and **civil rights** leader Dr. Martin Luther King Jr. heard what happened. He led a bus **boycott**. Parks's actions helped to end **segregation** in America's South. It was the beginning of a new era of the **Civil Rights movement.** Rosa Parks did not plan her historic act. "I did not get on the bus to get arrested," she has said. "I got on the bus to go home."

▲ Rosa Parks is often called the "Mother of the Civil Rights movement."

◆ ◆ ◆ ◆ ◆

---

boarded, got onto
refused, said no
arrested, took someone away because he or she did something wrong
civil rights, equal rights for all people
boycott, organized refusal to do something
segregation, the separation of whites and blacks
Civil Rights movement, political struggle from the 1950s to the 1970s

Albert Einstein (1879–1955) was a famous **physicist.** Einstein tried to find the answers to many questions about the **universe**.

When Einstein was a child, he did not seem especially smart. In fact, his parents worried because he learned to talk so late. He was also an underachiever at school. He hated going to classes and taking tests. He graduated from college but then couldn't find a teaching job. But he kept working on his mathematical **theories** even though people thought he wasn't smart. Later people realized he was a **genius.**

After Einstein died, scientists removed his brain. They found that Einstein's brain was unusual. Some parts were different and some were larger than average. These differences may have helped Einstein become such an extraordinary thinker.

◆ ◆ ◆ ◆ ◆

---

physicist, scientist who studies forces like heat, light, and movement
universe, everything that exists
theories, ideas that try to explain something
genius, someone who has extraordinary talents

▲ Albert Einstein is one of the most famous scientists in history.

BEFORE YOU GO ON . . .

1 Why was Rosa Parks arrested?
2 In what way was Albert Einstein's brain unusual?

HOW ABOUT YOU?
● Would you like to talk to Einstein or Parks? What questions would you ask them?

Stephen Hawking (1942–) is a famous physicist. He has a disease that affects his **nerves** and muscles. Hawking cannot walk. He is incapable of talking without a voice synthesizer—a special kind of computer that produces sound. However, his disability doesn't stop him from living an active life. Hawking travels, teaches, and writes books. He says that his disability gives him the freedom to think more about physics and the universe.

Hawking has written many science books, including *A Brief History of Time* and *The Universe in a Nutshell.* Many people think he is a genius.

◆　◆　◆　◆　◆

▲ Stephen Hawking uses a special wheelchair to get around.

Early in the twentieth century, the North Pole was still undiscovered. Many explorers wanted to be the first ones there. No one is certain, but **Robert Peary** (1856–1920) and **Matthew Henson** (1866–1955) were probably the first people to reach the North Pole. Both men **endured** dangerous conditions on their expedition. Traveling to the North Pole is very difficult because you have to walk across large areas of ice. Ice can break apart and move **without warning**. Both men fell into dangerous icy water and were rescued. But on April 6, 1909, they reached their **goal**—the North Pole— the very top of the world!

◆　◆　◆　◆　◆

▲ Peary (above) and Henson (below) traveled 644 kilometers (400 mi.) in 37 days.

nerves, parts of your body that control movement and feeling
endured, faced with courage
without warning, unexpectedly; unpredictably
goal, something that you want to achieve

When **Helen Keller** (1880–1968) was nineteen months old, she became sick with a **fever**. The sickness left her without sight or hearing. She couldn't see or hear. Because she was so young when she lost her sight and hearing, it was hard for her to learn to communicate. Also, because she could not see, she couldn't use sign language—the language of hearing-impaired people. She also couldn't "read lips," as many hearing-impaired people do. She was very **frustrated**. But she was extremely intelligent and learned different ways to communicate. For instance, she learned to understand speech by touching the speaker's lips and throat. She learned that everything had a name and that these names were words.

Keller gave lectures (with her teacher's help) and wrote many books.

◆ ◆ ◆ ◆ ◆

▲ Helen Keller was the first sight- and hearing-impaired person to graduate from college.

Wolfgang Amadeus Mozart (1756–1791) was born in Salzburg, Austria. When he was three years old, he began to play the harpsichord. When he was five, he wrote his first song.

◀ Mozart was a child genius.

Because of his unusual talent, Mozart had a very uncommon childhood. By the time he was six years old, he was traveling around Europe performing concerts for royal families. He became a brilliant musician and **composer**.

During Mozart's life, people didn't recognize his genius. He was extremely poor and not well known. Today, he is recognized as one of history's great composers. People everywhere still enjoy his music.

◆ ◆ ◆ ◆ ◆

---

fever, high temperature
frustrated, upset because you can't do something
composer, person who writes music

BEFORE YOU GO ON . . .

1. What did Robert Peary and Matthew Henson want to achieve?
2. In what ways was Mozart's childhood uncommon?

HOW ABOUT YOU?
- Would you prefer to be a scientist or a musician? Why?

53

Ellen Ochoa (1958–) has an extraordinary job. She is an astronaut—someone who travels in space. She studied physics and **engineering** in college. In 1987, she was in the top 100 out of 2,000 applicants to the National Aeronautics and Space Administration (NASA) space program. In 1990, NASA chose Ochoa and twenty-two others to begin training at the Johnson Space Center in Houston, Texas.

Ochoa has gone on three missions and has flown in space more than 700 hours. (This is the same as flying fourteen times to the moon and back.) In just one year (1999), she flew more than 11 million kilometers (7 million mi.) in space! Ochoa was the first Hispanic woman ever to become an astronaut. She tells students: "If you stay in school, you have the **potential** to achieve what you want in the future."

◆ ◆ ◆ ◆ ◆

▲ Astronaut Ellen Ochoa is also a musician!

▲ Adriana Fernandez won the New York City Marathon in 1999.

Adriana Fernandez (1971–) is a Mexican runner who is famous all over the world. In 1995, Fernandez won a gold medal at the Pan American Games. In 1996, she set a Mexican national record and won the Houston Tenneco event. Fernandez was injured, however, and lost her chance to compete at the Olympic Games in Atlanta in 1996.

But Fernandez didn't **give up**. In 1998, she finished in second place at the New York City Marathon. Finally, in November 1999, Fernandez won the New York City Marathon. She is the first Mexican woman to win this internationally known marathon.

◆ ◆ ◆ ◆ ◆

engineering, the science that plans the way machines, roads, etc., are built
potential, possibility; opportunity
give up, stop trying

Erik Weihenmayer (1968–) lost his sight when he was thirteen years old. Later he discovered that he was a **skilled** athlete. Weihenmayer can sky dive, wrestle, and ski. In 2001, Weihenmayer achieved his dream of climbing to the top of the highest mountain in the world—Mount Everest.

Since his climb, Weihenmayer has received hundreds of e-mails. "It's amazing, this response," he said. "It seems it woke up so many people. If you have the right talent and the right ability, you should be given the opportunity to do what you want to do in life. . . . I've never seen myself as a blind guy who climbs. I see myself as a mountaineer and I happen to be blind."

In September 2002, Weihenmayer achieved his ultimate goal of climbing all "seven summits"—the tallest mountains on each of the seven continents.

◆　◆　◆　◆　◆

---

skilled, capable; excellent

BEFORE YOU GO ON . . .

1 Why is Ellen Ochoa an extraordinary person?

2 In what way is Erik Weihenmayer unusual as a mountain climber?

HOW ABOUT YOU?

- Of the people you read about, which did you find most interesting? Why?

▼ Erik Weihenmayer climbing Mount Everest

Review and Practice

Each of the people you read about in "Extraordinary People" faced a challenge and made a choice. Copy this chart into your notebook. Then reread "Extraordinary People" and complete the chart.

Person	Challenge	Choice
Rosa Parks	She was an African American living in a segregated society.	She chose not to give her seat to a white person even though the driver said she would be arrested.
Albert Einstein		
Stephen Hawking		
Robert Peary and Matthew Henson		
Helen Keller		
Wolfgang Amadeus Mozart		
Ellen Ochoa		
Adriana Fernandez		
Erik Weihenmayer		

EXTENSION

Choose an extraordinary person you have read about. Draw a timeline of his or her life using the information you have. Think about:

- chronological events
- important dates
- challenges the person faced
- choices the person made

DISCUSSION

Discuss in pairs or small groups.

1. Which two people are physicists? What made them extraordinary?

2. Why is Rosa Parks's action so important in American history?

3. How is life challenging for a person with a physical disability, like Helen Keller, Stephen Hawking, or Erik Weihenmayer?

4. Intelligence, physical strength, determination, and creativity are all important qualities. Choose three people from "Extraordinary People." Which qualities does each have? Which quality do you think is the most important?

5. Do you know any extraordinary people? What makes them extraordinary? Compare the people you chose with those of your partner or group.

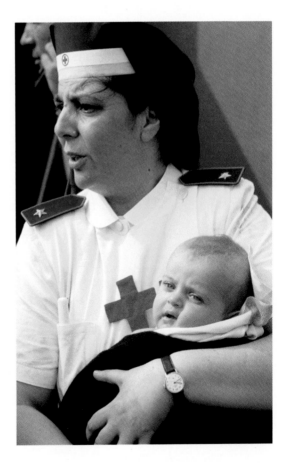

Personal Narrative

In this section, you will read a personal narrative. In a personal narrative, the narrator, or person telling the story, tells about something that he or she experienced. Because this narrative is about a real event, it is nonfiction. This experience took place near the end of World War II—in October 1945. Nazi Germany was occupying Holland.

He Was the Same Age as My Sister

Mieke C. Malandra

I'm nearly sixty-seven years old, but every October when the weather **turns**, I am eleven again.

In the last year of the war, fall in Holland was cold and wet. No lighted stoves, no coal. No lamps to make the room seem warm, no electricity. No supper worth the name. The soup from the central kitchen, a mixture of potato peels and cabbage leaves in water without salt, was cold by the time we got it home.

That day in October, just when it began to get dark, army trucks closed off our street, as they had done many times before, and a **platoon** of German soldiers started a house-to-house search for men.

"**Raus**! Raus!" The **loudspeaker** drove us outside to stand on the sidewalk while soldiers ran through our houses, poking in **attics** and closets. "Raus! Raus!" My little brothers forgot to grab their coats. Jacob's little body warmed me.

Our street filled up with women and children. We could talk freely, since the soldiers didn't understand Dutch, but we kept our voices low. Jokes flew around. I didn't understand what they were talking

---

turns, changes

HOLLAND

GERMANY

BELGIUM •— Maastricht

---

platoon, part of an army
Raus, German for "get out"
loudspeaker, piece of equipment that makes a person's voice louder
attics, rooms at the top of a house under the roof

about, but I liked the laughter. Then news
was exchanged. They're in Maastricht! Why
won't they come north?

It got colder. The soldiers had nearly
come to the end of the street, and no men
had been found. We became quiet. And
then we heard someone crying. All the
mothers turned. It was the sound of a
crying child. On the **stoop** of Mr. van
Campen's house sat a soldier, his rifle
propped up next to him, his face hidden in
his coat. He tried to swallow his **sobs**, but
then he gave up.

---

stoop, stairway or porch at the entrance of a house
sobs, the sounds someone makes when crying

LITERARY ELEMENT

The *mood* of a story is its atmosphere or feeling.
The mood can be sad, funny, scary, tense, happy,
hopeless, etc. Writers create mood with descriptive
language, by telling what people are doing or
saying, and what's happening.

BEFORE YOU GO ON . . .

1 How old is the narrator? How old is she
during the story?

2 Try to predict what the mothers will do.

HOW ABOUT YOU?

● Where do you think all the men in the
village have gone?

59

A mother walked over and talked to him softly in German. "What's wrong?" she asked. She bent over him as he spoke, and when he was finished, she stood straight up and **announced** to us, "This war must nearly be over. He's sixteen years old and hasn't had anything to eat today." Two or three mothers slipped away from the group and went into their houses. A German officer came walking down the street half a **block** away. I was scared—and very cold. The mothers managed to get back in time. A cold cooked potato, a piece of bread, and a wrinkled apple were passed through the group to the boy.

The officer came closer. The boy turned into a soldier again. "**Danke**," he said, and then climbed to his feet and grabbed his rifle.

The truck engines started up. We could go inside. For the rest of the war, for the rest of my life, I have remembered that soldier who cried. He was the same age as my sister.

announced, told
block, the distance between two streets
Danke, German for "thank you"

BEFORE YOU GO ON . . .

1. Why is the young German soldier crying?
2. What do the women in the town do? Why did they do it?

HOW ABOUT YOU?

• Did you feel sorry for the soldier? Why or why not?

Link the Readings

REFLECTION

Reread "He Was the Same Age as My Sister." Then copy the chart into your notebook. Look back at the texts and complete the chart.

Title of Selection	Type of Text (Genre)	Fiction or Nonfiction	Purpose of Selection	Something I Liked/Didn't Like About It
"Extraordinary People"			to inform	
"He Was the Same Age as My Sister"				

DISCUSSION

Discuss in pairs or small groups.

1. What is extraordinary about Rosa Parks? Discuss what she did.

2. What is special about the mothers in "He Was the Same Age as My Sister"? Discuss what they did.

3. Of the people you read about in Part 1, who would you most like to invite to your house for dinner? Why? What would you talk about?

4. Challenges can be big, like climbing a mountain,or small, like learning to ride a bike. What are some big or small challenges you have faced and the decisions you made?

Connect to Writing

GRAMMAR

Using the Simple Past

Use the **simple past** to talk about an action that happened in the past and is completed.

> In 2001, Erik Weihenmayer **climbed** Mount Everest.
> Helen Keller **graduated** from college.
> Adriana Fernandez **won** a gold medal in 1995.

Most verbs are regular. To form the simple past of most regular verbs, add **-ed** to the base form.

walk + -ed	**walked**	climb + -ed	**climbed**
play + -ed	**played**	fill + -ed	**filled**

For regular verbs that end with **-e**, add **-d** to the base to form the simple past.

close + -d	**closed**	graduate + -d	**graduated**
use + -d	**used**	recognize + -d	**recognized**

Some verbs are irregular. These verbs have special past forms.

eat	**ate**	keep	**kept**
have	**had**	is	**was**
go	**went**	fall	**fell**
come	**came**	think	**thought**
fly	**flew**	make	**made**
win	**won**	understand	**understood**

For negative simple past sentences, use ***did not (didn't)* + verb.**

> Albert Einstein **did not like** school very much.
> Rosa Parks **did not give** her seat to a white person.
> The German soldiers **didn't understand** Dutch.

Practice

Look through "Extraordinary People" and "He Was the Same Age as My Sister." Find ten sentences in the simple past. Write them in your notebook. Circle the verbs. Then compare sentences in pairs.

SKILLS FOR WRITING

Writing a Narrative Paragraph

Narrative writing tells a story. The story can be either fiction or nonfiction. If it is a story about something from the narrator's own experience, it is called personal narrative. The events are usually told in chronological order—that is, in the order that they happened. These sequence words show chronological order: *First, . . . Next, . . . After, . . . Then, . . . Finally, . . .*

   Read about Milica's grandparents. Then discuss the questions.

> Milica Bogetic
>
> ### My Amazing Grandparents
>
> My grandparents are amazing people. My grandfather was in the army for four years during World War II. *After* the war, he studied at the Sorbonne in Paris, and *then* went to Harvard and got a Ph.D. He met my grandmother there. They got married in December 1952. My grandfather taught at the University of Connecticut. He and my grandmother had three children, but the second child died. *Then* they adopted two more children. *After* that, my grandmother got a master's degree and worked as a part-time teacher and an editor. Both of my grandparents speak several languages. My grandmother taught English to immigrants. *After* my grandfather retired in 1992, he taught English to inmates at a prison.

sequence words

1. What makes this text a personal narrative?
2. What verbs does the writer use?
3. What words and phrases show chronological order?

WRITING ASSIGNMENT

Narrative Paragraph

You will write a narrative paragraph about an extraordinary person.

1. **Read** Choose a person you think is extraordinary. You can choose a famous person, a friend, or a family member.

Writing Strategy: Notes

Making notes is a good way to organize information before you write. Notes don't have to be in complete sentences. They can be words or phrases. Look at the notes the writer made before writing the paragraph about her grandparents.

> Grandfather—
>
> was in the army
>
> studied at the Sorbonne
>
> Grandfather and Grandmother—
>
> met at Harvard
>
> had 3 children, adopted 2 more
>
> were teachers
>
> speak several languages

1. What information from the notes did the writer include in her paragraph?

2. How is the format different from the paragraph on page 63?

2. **Make notes** In your notebook, make notes about your extraordinary person.

3. **Write** Use your notes to write a paragraph. Write your paragraph in the simple past.

EDITING CHECKLIST

Did you . . .

▶ indent the first sentence in your paragraph?

▶ place the events in chronological order?

▶ include the most important events?

▶ use the simple past?

▶ write in complete sentences?

▶ begin each sentence with a capital letter?

▶ end each sentence with a period?

PART REVIEW 1

Check Your Knowledge

Language Development

1. How can prefixes help you figure out word meaning?

2. What do you do when you skim a text?

3. What is one reason to make notes before you begin writing?

4. What is the mood of "He Was the Same Age as My Sister"? How does the author create mood in this story?

5. What are three sequence words we use in narrative writing?

6. What letters do you add to the base form of a regular verb to form the simple past? Write a sentence that tells something you did yesterday.

Academic Content

1. What new social studies vocabulary did you learn in Part 1? What do the words mean?

2. Choose one person described in "Extraordinary People." Describe the challenges he/she faced and choices he/she made.

3. What was happening in history at the time of the story "He Was the Same Age as My Sister"?

▲ A fork in the road

Prepare to Read

BACKGROUND

The novel *A Boat to Nowhere* is historical fiction. In most historical fiction, the setting and events are nonfictional but the characters are fictional. The historical background in this story is the Vietnam War during the 1960s and 1970s.

The excerpt from *A Boat to Nowhere* has many characters. This character chart will help you understand the story.

	Characters
Mai	an eleven-year-old orphan girl
Loc	Mai's younger brother
Thay Van Chi	Mai and Loc's grandfather and the village teacher
Tam and Duc	a couple who rescued Mai, Loc, and Thay Van Chi from the forest
Hong	the family's maid and cook
Kien	a fourteen-year-old orphan who has just arrived at Tam and Duc's home

Make connections Look at the map. Where is North Vietnam? Where is South Vietnam?

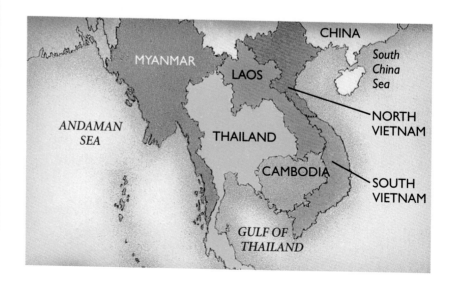

66

LEARN KEY WORDS

beggars
belly
memory
rags
rifles
run away

VOCABULARY

Read these sentences. Use the context to figure out the meaning of the **red** words. Use a dictionary to check your answers. Write each word and its meaning in your notebook.

1. **Beggars** ask others for food or money so they can survive.
2. Kien ate bowls of rice until his **belly** was full.
3. Mai's **memory** of losing her mother and father made her sad.
4. Hong burned the dirty old **rags** that Kien wore.
5. The soldiers used **rifles** to fight the enemy.
6. People in the village tried to **run away** from the soldiers.

READING STRATEGY

Visualizing

Visualizing means imagining, or picturing, the characters, events, and places in a text. Writers use descriptive words to help readers visualize. Usually the descriptive words are adjectives, but they can also be verbs or nouns:

- Kien's **narrow black** eyes were **unfriendly**. (adjectives)
- Your belly will **explode** if you eat more. (verb)
- We had a big **home** with **flowers** in the **garden**. (nouns)

Visualizing can help you understand and enjoy a text.

Vietnamese "boat people" arrive in Hong Kong. ▶

Historical Fiction

First, preview the excerpt from A Boat to Nowhere. Refer to the chart on page 66 to help you keep track of the characters. Then, as you read the text more carefully, visualize images that the adjectives, verbs, and nouns create. Which images are easy to visualize?

from A Boat to Nowhere

Maureen Crane Wartski

In their small, isolated village in South Vietnam, Mai and her family thought they were safe from the war. Then Kien, a fourteen-year-old **orphan,** *came into their lives, bringing tales of terrible conquerors from the North taking over the forest villages.*

Kien could certainly eat!

Mai watched amazed as the boy **wolfed down** four big bowls of rice and held out his bowl for more. Hong grumbled, but filled it up again. She said loudly that she was glad to cook and take care of Thay Van Chi and his family, but feeding a beggar brat she did not enjoy.

"If you're going to work for your rice as you boasted, you'll end up working for years!" she snapped in her loud voice.

Kien paid no attention. He slurped his rice, scooping it up into his mouth as if his

---

to nowhere, not to any place; with no destination
orphan, child whose parents have died
wolfed down, ate hungrily and quickly, like a wolf

chopsticks couldn't work fast enough. Mai couldn't help staring. Hadn't he ever learned any **manners?**

"What are you looking at?" Kien's narrow black eyes were unfriendly. "Haven't you ever seen a person eat?"

Mai **blushed.** "Grandfather wants to see you when you've eaten," she said. "He sent me to tell you."

"You'll have to wash first. No one is going to get near the teacher in your condition!" Hong insisted.

Kien gave a snort of laughter. "Too bad. I've grown fond of all my **lice and fleas,**" he said.

He held out his rice bowl again, but Hong shook her head. "Your belly will explode if you eat more. Now, here is soap and a towel. Over there is the bathing area. There is a large jug of fresh water. Do you hear me? Now, wash!" Kien shrugged. "Here are some clean clothes. The clothes may not fit, but beggars can't choose. I am going to burn those rags you're wearing. Now, move!"

---

manners, correct way to act
blushed, turned red with embarrassment
lice and fleas, small insects that live on people's or
  animals' skin or in their hair

BEFORE YOU GO ON . . .

1 Why does Kien eat so quickly?

2 Why does Hong say that Kien's belly will explode?

HOW ABOUT YOU?
- Do you like Hong? Why or why not?

Kien grinned **impudently**. "Sure, . . ." he said, and **sauntered off**. Hong's face turned a brick red.

"Imagine having to cook for such a one at this time of night!" she grumbled. "Here, Mai. Help me clean up!"

While Mai helped Hong in the cooking area behind the house she could hear Duc and Big Tam talking with Grandfather. Mai caught the words "Kien" and "bad" and "he should go away."

"They don't want Kien to stay in the Village," Mai said to Hong. "Why?"

"He's a bad boy. Besides, he doesn't **belong** here."

"Loc and I weren't born in the Village," Mai pointed out. "Grandfather brought us here when Loc was just a baby. But *we* belong here!"

"That's different." Hong's face softened, and she turned to smooth back Mai's black hair. "From the time Tam and Duc found you in the forest, you and Loc have been like my own."

Mai nodded, remembering how kind this big, rough woman had been . . . how kind everyone else had been. The Village had **taken them to their hearts**, and soon Thay Van Chi had become the Village's **revered** teacher and its headman. Then why . . .

"Why doesn't anyone like Kien?" Mai wanted to know. "Is it because he's so rude?"

"That and other reasons."

---

impudently, rudely; disrespectfully
sauntered off, walked away
belong, be connected to or part of a place
taken them to their hearts, welcomed them
revered, greatly respected

What other reasons could there be? Mai wondered.

Hong began to busy herself **stacking** newly washed pots. Then she stopped to ask, "Mai, do you remember very much about your first home? In the city, I mean, when your parents still lived?"

Mai said, "I remember Mama and Father—a little. Mama was very pretty. She was always singing to me and playing with me. Father was a doctor. We had a big home with flowers in the garden. I was named for the flowers. . . ."

"Do you remember why you left the city?" Hong asked.

"Father had to go away to be a doctor to the soldiers. He . . . he never came back." Even now the memory hurt Mai so much she hurried over this part. "Mama and I went to live with Grandfather in another city. Then Mama went to the hospital and Loc was born." Mai's voice **dropped to a whisper**. "Mama never came back from the hospital. . . ."

"Ah," Hong said, her eyes full of tears.

"Grandfather said that the war had killed both Father and Mama. He took Loc and me away from the city. Loc was just a little baby and he cried a lot." Mai remembered that she had often cried herself as they walked hour after hour, from one town to another.

LITERARY ELEMENT

A *flashback* interrupts the action in narrative fiction. It tells about something in the past. It gives the reader a more complete picture of a character or the current situation.

---

stacking, placing in a pile
dropped to a whisper, became very quiet

BEFORE YOU GO ON . . .

1 How does Hong feel about Mai and her brother, Loc?

2 Who did Mai and Loc live with before they came to the village?

HOW ABOUT YOU?

• Does this part of the story help you visualize? What images come to your mind?

Each time they arrived at a new village or town she had asked her grandfather whether they could stay there, but Thay Van Chi had kept on going.

"It took us a long, long time to reach the Village," Mai told Hong. "I don't know how many towns and villages we stayed in . . . and we were often lost. One day we were so lost in the forest that I was sure we'd never find our way. Then Tam and Duc found us. . . ."

There was a silence. Mai could hear Kien **scrubbing** himself some distance away in the bathing area. He sang as he **sluiced** water over himself:

"Oh, rifles are coming closer, my sister—
*Ah, the **cannon** is **booming**, Mother!*
Why don't you take your baby and run
    away?"

"Stop that noise!" Hong shouted. Mai saw that the big woman was shaking, and suddenly she, too, was afraid. Why was Kien singing of rifles and cannon and running away? Why had Hong asked her to remember the old days?

"What has my remembering about the city to do with Kien not being welcome in the Village?" she asked.

Hong **grunted**. "You ask too many questions," she said in her normal voice. "Go away now. I'm too busy to talk to you."

---

scrubbing, rubbing with a cloth or brush
sluiced, washed with water
cannon, large gun, usually on wheels
booming, making loud noises
grunted, made a short, low sound

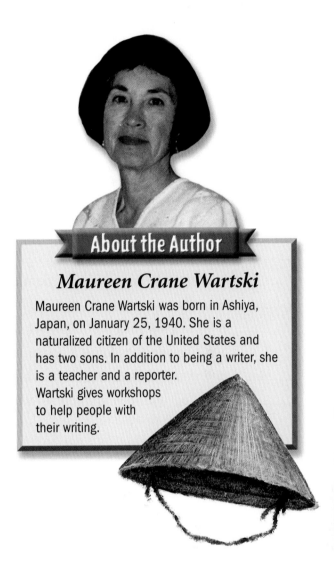

About the Author

Maureen Crane Wartski

Maureen Crane Wartski was born in Ashiya, Japan, on January 25, 1940. She is a naturalized citizen of the United States and has two sons. In addition to being a writer, she is a teacher and a reporter. Wartski gives workshops to help people with their writing.

BEFORE YOU GO ON . . .

1. In Kien's song, why should the mother "run away"?
2. How does Kien's song make Hong and Mai feel?

HOW ABOUT YOU?

- Do you like Kien? Would you like to know him? Why or why not?

Review and Practice

Reread the excerpt from *A Boat to Nowhere*. Number the events in chronological order. Remember that some of these events took place before Mai and Loc arrived at the village. Write the sentences in your notebook.

_____ Hong gives Kien food and Mai watches him eat it.

_____ Hong makes Kien take a bath.

_____ The villagers say they don't want Kien to stay.

_____ Grandfather brings Mai and Loc to the new village.

_____ Kien sings a song that frightens Hong.

___1___ Mai's father goes to be a doctor for the soldiers.

_____ The villagers welcome Mai, her brother, and their grandfather.

_____ Mai, Loc, and their grandfather walk for a very long time and get lost in the forest.

Use the list to retell the story to a partner.

EXTENSION

Copy the Venn diagram into your notebook. Reread the story and look at the
list of characters on page 66. Fill in the missing characters in Mai's past and
present (before and after she came to the village). Which characters are in
both Mai's past and present?

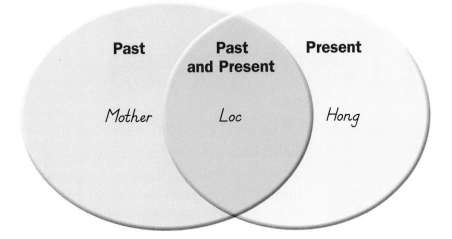

DISCUSSION

Discuss in pairs or small groups.

1. Why do you think Mai has many memories of living in the city?

2. Do you like this story? Do you want to read the rest?

3. Why don't the villagers want Kien to stay?

4. What do you think will happen next in the story?

Social Studies

This is a magazine article about real people and events. Preview and skim the text. With your classmates, make some predictions about what the article is about. Write them on the chalkboard. Then, in your notebook, write two questions that you think the article will answer. Think of the questions as you read the article.

Sudan's "Lost Boys" Start New Lives

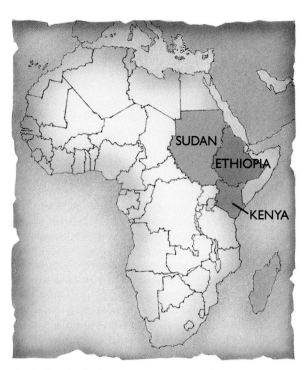

▲ Sudan is the largest country in Africa.

Since the mid-1980s, the people of Sudan have experienced terrible **civil war** caused by religious, **ethnic**, and regional **conflict**. In 1987 and 1988, about 20,000 boys and 2,000 girls left their villages in southern Sudan. They left because their villages were destroyed by **troops** from the northern Khartoum government. Most adults and girls were killed or sold as **slaves**. The boys, mostly between five and ten years old, had nowhere to go and no one to take care of them. They walked hundreds of kilometers through the East African desert. Some boys carried their baby brothers as they walked. Many died of hunger, thirst, disease, or attack by wild animals. To stay alive, they often ate leaves and mud.

---

civil war, war between two or more groups of people who live in the same country
ethnic, racial or cultural
conflict, fight or argument
troops, soldiers; members of the army
slaves, people who are sold for money

▲ David Akuei, wearing new clothes, leaves a mud hut in Kenya to travel to the United States.

About 12,000 children reached Ethiopia. In Ethiopia, and later in Kenya, they lived in **refugee camps** for over ten years. They didn't have any parents, so the children formed their own "family" groups. The older children took care of the younger ones. **Relief workers** in the camps named the children the "Lost Boys." This name comes from the book *Peter Pan*. In *Peter Pan*, a group of boys stays together without adults.

---

refugee camps, temporary living areas for people who
   have to leave their homes because of war
relief workers, people who help victims of a disaster

Now most of these "lost boys" are young men between seventeen and twenty-five years old. About 4,000 of them have moved to the United States. First, the young men fly from Kenya to the United States. Then they go to cities across the United States. Relief **organizations** are helping the men start a new life in freedom and safety.

One organization, World Vision, is helping about fifty young Sudanese men **settle** in the Seattle area of Washington. World Vision first places each young man with an American family for two to four weeks. Then the young men move into apartments. They study English and learn about American culture. They must learn all **aspects** of American life (from using a can opener to finding a job) very quickly. That way, they can learn to live **independently**. This is a very difficult task, especially when they have never seen mattresses, lightbulbs, ice, or a television.

---

organizations, groups such as clubs or businesses
settle, begin to live in a new place
aspects, parts of a situation, idea, problem, etc.
independently, alone, without help

BEFORE YOU GO ON . . .

1 Why did the "Lost Boys" of Sudan have to leave their homes?
2 How did these boys get to Ethiopia?

HOW ABOUT YOU?
- Do you know the story of Peter Pan? If not, do you know any stories about children like the "lost boys"?

Since they arrived, the young men have been amazed by new discoveries: keys, stoves, stairs, and telephones. Then there is macaroni, canned juice, and the "huge white box" in the kitchen. They tried lifting the strange machine from the bottom. They tried pulling it apart. Then they discovered the handle and opened the refrigerator. It was full of cold, unfamiliar foods.

Some of the young men will use their time in the United States to get a good education and earn money. Then they hope to return to Sudan and rebuild their villages.

▲ Philip Maliah Dar (right) is congratulated by his teacher in an English class at Harvard University.

BEFORE YOU GO ON . . .

1 What were some things that surprised the young men?

2 What did they do with the refrigerator?

HOW ABOUT YOU?

• What did you find interesting about the "lost boys'" experience?

▲ Mou Deng reaches up to catch a snowflake in front of his new home in the United States.

Link the Readings

Reread "Sudan's 'Lost Boys' Start New Lives." Then think about it and the excerpt from *A Boat to Nowhere* as you look at the chart. Copy the chart into your notebook and complete it.

Title of Selection	Type of Text (Genre)	Fiction or Nonfiction	Purpose of Selection	Country/Countries
From *A Boat to Nowhere*		fiction		Vietnam
"Sudan's 'Lost Boys' Start New Lives"	magazine article		to inform	

DISCUSSION

Discuss in pairs or small groups.

1. Which text did you prefer, the excerpt from *A Boat to Nowhere* or "Sudan's 'Lost Boys' Start New Lives"? Did you prefer it because of the style, the people, or for some other reason? Explain.

2. Compare the lives of the orphans in the excerpt from *A Boat to Nowhere* and "Sudan's 'Lost Boys' Start New Lives." In what ways are their lives similar and different? What kind of challenges do they face? What kind of choices can they make?

3. What objects that we see every day in the United States might be different for people from Vietnam or Sudan?

4. Imagine you have to describe an everyday object, such as a table or an umbrella, to someone who doesn't know what that object is. Describe what the object does and how it works.

▲ Two students take a break from English lessons to work on their soccer skills.

Connect to Writing

GRAMMAR

Using the Conjunction *but*

The **conjunction *but*** connects two contrasting ideas. Use *but* to connect two contrasting adjectives.

> Kien's new clothes were clean. Kien's new clothes were ragged.
> Kien's new clothes were clean **but** ragged.

Use *but* to combine two contrasting simple sentences. The combined sentence is called a compound sentence. A compound sentence usually has a comma before the conjunction.

> Kien ate several bowls of rice. He was still hungry.
> Kien ate several bowls of rice, **but** he was still hungry.

Practice

Copy these simple sentence pairs into your notebook. Then combine each pair using the conjunction *but*.

Examples:

> The day was hot. The day was windy.
> The day was hot **but** windy.

> The "lost boys" didn't know English. They are learning quickly.
> The "lost boys" didn't know English, **but** they are learning quickly.

1. The village was small. The village was crowded.
2. The "lost boys" didn't have much food. They were grateful for what they had.
3. Many children died in Sudan. Twelve thousand survived.
4. Kien slept for twelve hours. He was still tired.
5. The boat was old. The boat was seaworthy.
6. Kien liked Loc and Mai. He didn't like Hong.

SKILLS FOR WRITING

Using a Variety of Sentence Types

Writers use different types of sentences to make their writing more interesting. For example, they use both simple sentences and compound sentences.

> **Simple sentence**
> Hong took care of Mai.
> **Compound sentence**
> Hong was glad to cook for Mai, but she did not want to cook for Kien.

Read the personal narrative. Then answer the questions about the paragraph.

Jennifer Rosario

My Big Challenge

Recently, I decided to try out for the Color Guard team at school. I had never done it before, but I decided to practice. ← simple sentence

First, we did difficult stretches, but I am not very flexible. ← compound sentence
Then, we worked with the flags, but I'm short and the tosses and the rotations were hard. I was so frustrated, I felt like giving up. I thought I would never succeed, but I kept practicing. I was determined to get better. Finally, the day of the tryouts arrived. I was so scared, I almost didn't go. I did my best. I didn't make the team, but I learned not to give up. Maybe I'll succeed next year.

1. How many simple sentences are there? How many compound sentences?
2. Is the first sentence interesting? Why or why not?
3. What does the writer do in this paragraph to make the writing interesting?

WRITING ASSIGNMENT

Personal Narrative

You will write a paragraph about a challenge you faced and what you learned from the experience.

1. **Read** Reread the model on page 81. How do you know that the writer felt challenged? What clues does the writer include to help you know how she felt?

Writing Strategy: Timeline

A timeline will help you place the events in chronological order. Look at this timeline of the events in "My Big Challenge."

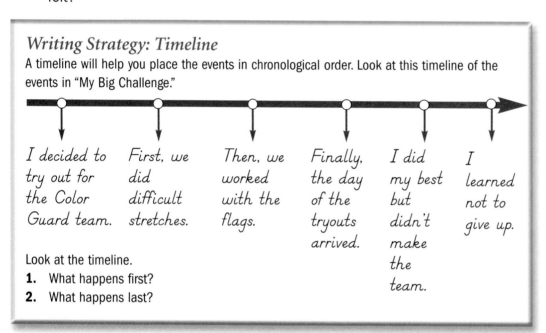

I decided to try out for the Color Guard team.

First, we did difficult stretches.

Then, we worked with the flags.

Finally, the day of the tryouts arrived.

I did my best but didn't make the team.

I learned not to give up.

Look at the timeline.
1. What happens first?
2. What happens last?

2. **Make a timeline** Think about a challenge you faced. Make a timeline in your notebook. Use the timeline to organize the material into chronological order.

3. **Write** Use your timeline and the model on page 81 to help you write about your experience.

EDITING CHECKLIST

Did you . . .

▶ tell the events in your story in chronological order?

▶ give enough details so that readers get a clear picture in their minds?

▶ use a variety of sentence types?

▶ use correct punctuation?

▶ indent the first sentence?

Check Your Knowledge

Language Development

1. What words does the author use to help you visualize Kien eating in the excerpt from *A Boat to Nowhere*?
2. Which part of the excerpt from *A Boat to Nowhere* is a flashback?
3. How can a timeline help you write about something that happened to you?
4. Give an example of a sentence that uses *but* to join two contrasting ideas.
5. Why is it important to use a variety of sentences in your writing?

Academic Content

1. What new social studies vocabulary did you learn in Part 2? What do the words mean?
2. What do you know about the Vietnam War?
3. What are some ways that the civil war in Sudan has changed the lives of the Sudanese people?

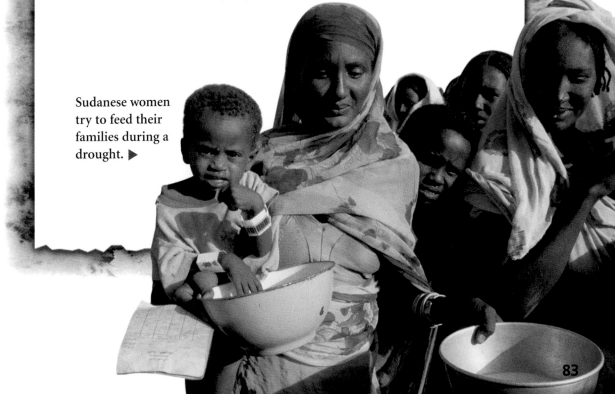

Sudanese women try to feed their families during a drought. ▶

Put It All Together

OBJECTIVES

Integrate Skills
- Listening/
  Speaking:
  *Panel
  discussion*
- Writing:
  *Personal
  narrative*

**Investigate
Themes**
- Projects
- Further
  reading

LISTENING and SPEAKING WORKSHOP

PANEL DISCUSSION

You will organize and present a panel discussion about the meaning of the word *challenge*.

1 **Think about it** Make a list of the challenges you read about in this unit. Make another list of challenges you have faced in your life. Read the examples in your two lists. Think about how to define the word *challenge*, and then write a definition.

Work in groups of four. Compare your lists and definitions. Discuss your ideas.

2 **Organize** Organize a panel discussion. Work together to define the word *challenge*. Use ideas from your group members' definitions. Include examples of challenges you read about or challenges you faced to support your definition. Write down your group's definition and supporting examples.

Each group member should plan to tell about a personal challenge from his or her life that illustrates your group's definition.

3 **Practice** Practice your panel discussion. One group member should present your group's definition of *challenge*. Then other group members should take turns telling about a personal challenge. After each person speaks, the other members of the panel can ask the speaker questions or make comments.

SPEAKING TIPS

- Speak loudly and clearly.
- Look at your audience as you speak.

4 **Present and evaluate** Present your panel discussion to your class. After each panel finishes, evaluate the presentation. What did you like best about the presentation? Do you have suggestions for improvement?

LISTENING TIP

If you don't understand something a speaker says, make a note. Wait until the speaker has finished and then ask your question.

WRITING WORKSHOP

PERSONAL NARRATIVE

In a personal narrative, the writer tells a story about events or people in his or her life. The story is about the writer's personal experience. Usually, the story includes a problem or difficult choice that the writer had to face or make.

A good personal narrative includes the following characteristics:

- a first-person narrator—or "I"—that tells the story
- a clear sequence of events in chronological order
- a problem or difficult choice the narrator faces
- a conclusion that tells how the narrator resolves the problem

You will write a personal narrative about a problem or difficult choice you faced and what you did to resolve the problem. Use the following steps and the model on page 86 to help you.

1 **Prewrite** Think about a problem or difficult choice you have faced. It can be a choice about a friend or something that happened at school or home. Make notes about it. Where were you? Who was there? What was the problem? What happened as a result of your choice? Read through your notes and then number them in chronological order.

WRITING TIP

Use sequence words to make the time periods and sequence of events clear to the reader. Sequence words usually appear at the beginning or end of a sentence. They show:
- a sequence, or order, of events: first, next, then, last, finally
- movement from one time period to another: before, after, later, while, during
- expressions of time: yesterday, last night, in 1998, on May 24, tomorrow, next week

Before you write a first draft of your personal narrative, read the following model. Notice the characteristics of a personal narrative.

Kate Younkins

Which Best Friend?

Sometimes I make plans that I forget. This is what happened with my two best friends last week. (First,) my friend Rachel called me up and invited me over to her house. I told her I could come. (Then) my friend Jena telephoned and invited me over to her house. Jena had just returned from her vacation in Florida. I hadn't seen Jena for a while, so I really wanted to see her. Without thinking, I said yes.

(After) I hung up the phone, I realized my problem. Now I had two plans for the same time with two different people. I felt bad. I wanted to see Rachel, but I hadn't seen Jena for a long time. I didn't know what to do.

(Finally,) I called each of them and invited them to come to my house. I explained to them what had happened. They thought it was funny!

The writer uses sequence words to make the time periods and sequence of events clear.

She describes her choice and how she felt about it.

Her conclusion tells how she resolved the problem.

2 **Draft** Use the model and your notes to write your personal narrative.

- Start your narrative in an interesting way, so your reader will want to read your story. Describe the characters and introduce your problem or difficult choice. Notice how the student starts her model narrative. How does she get you interested in her story?

- Describe your problem or choice in the next paragraph. Tell how you felt about the situation.

- Conclude your narrative by describing what you did to resolve the problem. If possible, explain what you learned from this experience.

3 **Edit** Work in pairs. Trade papers and read each other's personal narratives. Use the questions in the editing checklist to evaluate each other's work.

> ### EDITING CHECKLIST
> #### Did you . . .
> ▶ write about events in the order that they happened?
> ▶ use sequence words to help the reader follow the chronology of what happened?
> ▶ capitalize the first letter of every sentence?
> ▶ use correct punctuation?
> ▶ use adjectives to express your feelings?

4 **Revise** Revise your personal narrative. Add ideas and correct mistakes, if necessary.

5 **Publish** Share your writing with your teacher and classmates.

PROJECTS

Work in pairs or small groups. Choose one of these projects.

1 Find out more about World War II, the Vietnam War, or the Sudanese civil war on the Internet. Share your findings with the class.

2 Work with a partner. One partner role plays one of the people in "Extraordinary People." The other partner interviews the person. Ask and answer these questions: *Who are you? What challenges have you faced? What makes you extraordinary?* Take turns playing each role. Present the interview to the class.

3 Choose an art material that you like to work with, such as paint, clay, colored pencils, or paper and glue. Look through the stories you read in this unit. Choose a setting, a character, or an event. Make some artwork showing what you chose. When you're finished, write a sentence or two about your artwork. Present your artwork and writing to the class.

4 Over the course of a few days, take note of daily challenges you face. Record the steps you go through as you meet each challenge. Compare your steps with those of a partner, and evaluate the steps. Were they effective? Sometimes effective? How can you improve them?

5 A collage is a kind of artwork that is made by cutting and pasting together different materials—for example, photos, drawings, written or typed words, or pictures. Some famous artists who made collages are Pablo Picasso, Georges Braque, and Henri Matisse. Find examples of their collages in library books or on the Internet.

Make a collage about yourself—a combination of words and pictures that shows who you are, what your interests are, and what challenges you have faced.

- Use words and pictures from newspapers, magazines, personal photos, your own writing or drawings.

- Cut and paste the pieces onto a piece of paper or cardboard.

- You can have your name in your collage or not, as you choose.

Share your collage with your class.

Further Reading

To find out more about the theme of this unit, choose from these reading suggestions.

Extreme Sports, **Richard Platt** Why do some people choose to go whitewater rafting down a wild river, parachute from an airplane, inline-skate on ramps and rails, or ski on steep mountainsides? What motivates them? Is it the thrill of a challenge, overcoming fears, proving they can master the world's most difficult sports, or something else?

Flying Ace: The Story of Amelia Earhart, **Angela Bull** Amelia Earhart was a very courageous pilot. In the 1920s, flying was rough and dangerous. Planes were unsafe and crashed often. But this didn't stop Earhart from wanting to fly. She bought her first plane when she was twenty-four years old. Seven years later, in 1928, she became the first woman to fly across the Atlantic Ocean.

Antarctic Adventure: Exploring the Frozen Continent, **Meredith Hooper** The history of the exploration of Antarctica is filled with victory and defeat. The men who first explored Antarctica 100 years ago sailed in wooden ships and struggled to keep warm. They had amazing, terrifying adventures. Why did they choose to explore such a difficult place? These stories testify to the courage of the human spirit.

Romeo and Juliet, **William Shakespeare** This is one of the most famous love stories of all time. The play is set in Verona, Italy, more than 400 years ago. Two important families—the Capulets (Juliet's family) and the Montagues (Romeo's family)—are longtime enemies. In spite of this, Romeo and Juliet fall in love, and their love ends their families' hate, but at a very high cost.

The House on Mango Street, **Sandra Cisneros** Esperanza Cordero is a young girl growing up in the Latino section of Chicago. Her life is full of heartbreak and joy. Her neighborhood is one of harsh realities and harsh beauty. She doesn't want to belong to this world and its low expectations of her. So she must invent for herself what she will become.

UNIT 3

Mysterious Ways

PART 1

- "Fact or Fiction?"
- "Truth or Lies?" George Shannon

PART 2

- "Teenage Detectives," Carol Farley and Elizabeth Dearl
- "How to Make a Friend Disappear" and "Water Trick"

A mystery is something that is hard to explain or understand. In a mystery story, there is a problem to solve, or figure out. The characters in the story—and you, the reader—get clues, or hints, to solve the problem.

In Part 1, you will read an article about some historical mysteries. Is there a monster in a lake in Scotland? What are "lost cities"? Is there really a curse on King Tutankhamen's tomb? You will also read three short mystery stories. In each story, you will get clues to solve the mystery.

In Part 2, you will read three short stories about two cousins who solve mysteries in their neighborhood. In the final reading, you will learn about two science experiments that make mysterious things happen.

Prepare to Read

BACKGROUND

"Fact or Fiction?" is a collection of mysteries that have puzzled people for centuries. They are nonfiction.

One such mystery concerns the Egyptian pyramids. These were monuments to the kings and queens who were buried inside them. About fifty pyramids have survived. How did the Egyptians lift the huge blocks to the top of the structures?

Make connections Look at the picture and some facts about the Great Pyramid at Giza in Egypt. Then discuss the questions.

The pyramid is as tall as a forty-story building.

It is made up of more than 2 million blocks of stone.

Each block weighs about 2,200 kilograms (5,000 lb.)—about the weight of a car.

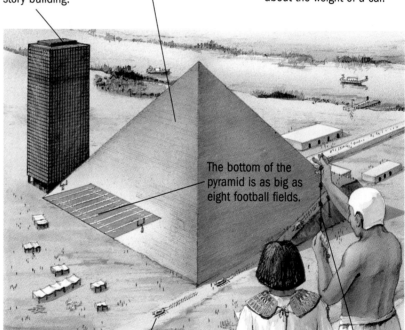

The bottom of the pyramid is as big as eight football fields.

20,000 workers took twenty years to build it.

Workers used logs and ramps.

Workers used a knotted string as a measurement tool.

1. What tools did the builders use to build the pyramids?
2. How do you think workers used logs and ramps to build the pyramids?
3. If a football field is 4,200 square meters (5,000 sq. yd.), how big is the bottom of the pyramid?

archaeologist
clues
creature
disappeared
fantasy
sacred

VOCABULARY

Read these sentences. Use the context to figure out the meaning of the **red** words. Use a dictionary to check your answers. Write each word and its meaning in your notebook.

1. The **archaeologist** dug in the ground and discovered an ancient Egyptian tomb.
2. Fingerprints and other **clues** helped the police find the criminal.
3. The **creature** was an unusual animal with six legs and no eyes.
4. No one knows why dinosaurs **disappeared** millions of years ago.
5. Scientists think that the monster isn't real but a **fantasy**.
6. A church, a temple, and a mosque are three kinds of **sacred** buildings.

READING STRATEGY

Distinguishing Fact and Opinion

A **fact** is a statement that someone can prove because there is evidence. It can be checked in such sources as textbooks or encyclopedias. An **opinion** is the statement of a belief, which cannot be proved. For example, the statement "The Incas built the city of Machu Picchu in Peru" is a fact because historical evidence proves it is true. However, the statement "Some archaeologists believe that the Incas left Machu Picchu because of smallpox, a deadly disease" is an opinion because it cannot be proved. No one knows for sure why the Incas left Machu Picchu.

How can you distinguish between fact and opinion?

- **For facts:** Ask yourself, "Can this statement be proved?"
- **For opinions:** Look for such words as: *believe, think, feel, might, perhaps.*

Science, Social Studies

As you read, try to distinguish what is a fact and what is an opinion.

Fact or Fiction?

Path to the Stars?

About 4,500 years ago, the **pharaoh** Cheops and his son and grandson built the three Pyramids of Giza in Egypt. These pyramids were tombs, or places to bury the dead. For thousands of years, people didn't understand why these three pyramids were grouped together.

Then Belgian **engineer** Robert Bauval noticed that the shape of the three pyramids was the same as part of a group of stars in the sky called Orion's Belt. The whole group of stars—Orion—was sacred to the Egyptians. When Cheops died, he was buried in the Great Pyramid of Giza. The Egyptians made a shaft—or hole—in this pyramid. The shaft led from Cheops's tomb to the sky and the stars of Orion. Scientists believe that the Egyptians built this shaft so Cheops could fly from the pyramid to Orion. There, he would become a god.

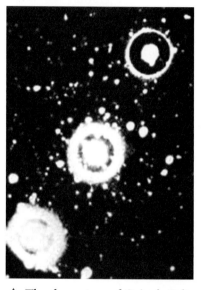

▲ The three stars of Orion's Belt

pharaoh, ancient Egyptian ruler
engineer, person who plans how to build machines, roads, etc.

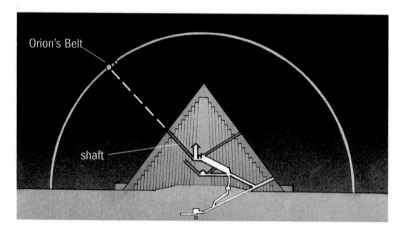

Orion's Belt

shaft

▲ The three Pyramids of Giza from high above

The Secret of the Sphinx

How old is the Sphinx? This question is one of the world's great mysteries. For thousands of years, wind and sand have **eroded** the Sphinx. Some archaeologists believe that water also damaged the Sphinx many **centuries** ago. Was the Sphinx once buried at the bottom of the sea? We don't know.

Mysterious Cities

Some ancient cities were abandoned and no one knows why. One of these cities is Machu Picchu, located about 2,440 meters (8,000 ft.) high in the Andes Mountains of Peru. The Incas built Machu Picchu from about 1460 to 1470 C.E. The Incas lived in parts of South America, including what is now Peru. They used stone blocks to build most of the buildings. The blocks fit together perfectly.

In the early 1500s, everyone left the city. No one knows why. Perhaps people died or left because of smallpox, a deadly disease that was brought by the Spanish. Machu Picchu was forgotten for hundreds of years. Then, in 1911, the American explorer Hiram Bingham rediscovered it. Today, **tourists** from all over the world visit this **unique** city.

---

eroded, slowly destroyed
centuries, periods of 100 years
tourists, people who travel for pleasure
unique, the only one of its type

▲ The Sphinx has the head of a man and the body of a lion.

BEFORE YOU GO ON . . .

1. Why do scientists think the Egyptians made a shaft in the Great Pyramid?
2. What has happened to the Sphinx over time?

HOW ABOUT YOU?

- Why do you think people might leave a city?

Stonehenge

Stonehenge is a mysterious monument of huge stones in England. Ancient peoples built Stonehenge about 5,000 years ago. No one really knows who these people were or why they built the monument.

Some people believe that Stonehenge was a **temple** to the sun. Other people believe that Stonehenge was a great stone calendar or **calculator**. They think the stones were arranged to measure the sun's movements, such as the summer and winter solstices—the longest and shortest days of the year. Perhaps Stonehenge was created to mark the rise of the sun and moon throughout the centuries. We may never know for sure.

▲ Some stones of Stonehenge came from 480 kilometers (300 mi.) away. How people moved them is a mystery.

Island of Giants

Easter Island is a tiny island in the Pacific Ocean, 3,620 kilometers (2,250 mi.) off the coast of Chile. It was named by Dutch explorers who arrived there on Easter Sunday, 1722. The island is covered with nearly 900 large **statues**, called "moai." Scientists believe they are the gods of the ancient people of Easter Island—the Rapa Nui people. But no one knows for sure. Another mystery is how the Rapa Nui people moved the heavy stones as far as 23 kilometers (14 mi.).

Archaeologists have found wooden tablets with the ancient language of the Rapa Nui people on it. No one knows how to read this language today. So the history of the Rapa Nui people is also a mystery. Only their great stone statues remain to watch over the island.

▲ The average height of a "moai" is 4 meters (13 ft.).

temple, holy building
calculator, instrument used to figure out mathematical problems
statues, shapes of people or animals made of stone, metal, or wood

Curse of the Pharaoh

Tutankhamen was a pharaoh in ancient Egypt. When he died, Tutankhamen was buried in a tomb with gold and other treasures.

In 1922, a group led by British archaeologists Howard Carter and Lord Carnarvon opened the tomb of Tutankhamen. They found many treasures, including a beautiful gold mask. Some people believed that a **message** carved in the tomb wall said, "Death will **slay** with his wings whoever disturbs the peace of the pharaoh." Lord Carnarvon died soon after opening the tomb. According to one story, Carnarvon's dog died at the same time at his home in England. Then, five months after Carnarvon died, his younger brother died suddenly.

According to one report, six of the twenty-six people at the opening of Tutankhamen's tomb died within ten years. However, many other people who were there lived to be very old. Was there really a curse?

---

curse, wish that something bad happens to someone
message, information that is sent to someone
slay, kill

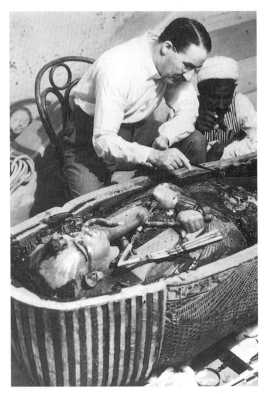

▲ Howard Carter and Tutankhamen's mummy

▲ Tutankhamen's mask

BEFORE YOU GO ON . . .

1. What is mysterious about Stonehenge and Easter Island?

2. What is the "curse of the pharaoh"?

HOW ABOUT YOU?

- What are two facts you learned about the pyramids, Stonehenge, or Easter Island? What are two opinions?

Terrifying Tentacles

Scientists say we know more about Mars than we do about the mysteries at the bottom of the ocean. Giant octopuses and squid are one of those mysteries. **Octopuses** and **squid** are usually only about 60 to 90 centimeters (2–3 ft.) long. However, there are reports of bigger creatures with tentacles long enough to pull a ship underwater. In 1753, a man in Norway described a huge sea monster "full of arms" that was big enough to crush a large ship. More recently, giant squid have been discovered with tentacles 10 meters (33 ft.) long. Imagine eating **calamari rings** the size of truck tires!

Scary Monsters

Most people believe that dinosaurs disappeared millions of years ago. However, a few dinosaurs may have survived. The famous Loch Ness monster may be a living dinosaur-like reptile called a plesiosaur.

People first reported seeing the Loch Ness monster in April 1933 when a new road was built on the north shore of Loch Ness, a lake in Scotland. A man and woman saw a huge creature with two black **humps** swimming across the lake. Then two more people saw a strange animal crossing the road with a sheep in its mouth. There is now a Loch Ness Investigation Bureau, but most scientists believe that the Loch Ness monster is a fantasy.

***

tentacles, long arm-like parts
octopuses, sea creatures with eight long tentacles
squid, sea creatures with a long body and ten tentacles
calamari rings, sliced squid, often served fried or in a salad
humps, raised parts on the back of an animal

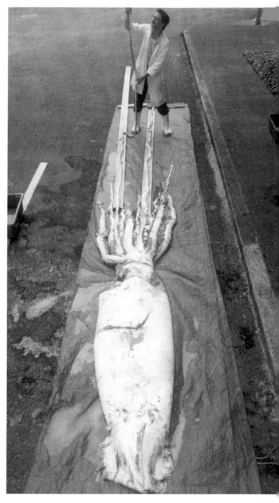

▲ A giant squid caught in the deep ocean off New Zealand. Giant squid live about 550 meters (1,800 ft.) beneath the sea.

This famous photograph of the Loch Ness monster is not authentic. The photographer tied a plastic head to a toy submarine. ▶

◀ Bigfoot and Yeti
look like giant apes.

Bigfoot and Yeti

There are stories about large ape-like creatures in **various** parts of the world. Different cultures give the creature different names. In the United States, for example, this creature is called Bigfoot or Sasquatch. In Tibet, it is called a yeti.

The first reports of Bigfoot date back to 1811. At that time, a man reported seeing footprints 36 centimeters (14 in.) long. In 1924, another man claimed that Bigfoot had kidnapped him. Each year many people in the United States claim to see Bigfoot. They often report seeing the creature in the forests of the Northwest.

Reports of a huge creature frightened the first European travelers in Tibet. (In Tibet, the word *yeti* means "manlike creature.") In 1951, a Mount Everest explorer found giant footprints in the snow.

Are there really creatures like the yeti and Bigfoot, or are they just stories? Bernard Heuvelmans (1916–1973), a famous **zoologist**, believed that the world is full of creatures still unknown to science. What do you think?

BEFORE YOU GO ON . . .

1 Do most scientists believe that the Loch Ness monster is real or a fantasy?

2 In the United States, where is Bigfoot usually seen?

HOW ABOUT YOU?

- Do you believe mysterious animals like the yeti or Loch Ness monster exist? What is your opinion?

---

various, different
zoologist, scientist who studies animals

Review and Practice

Reread "Fact or Fiction?" Then copy the chart into your notebook. Make a quiz for your classmates. Write one question in the chart about each of the mysteries. Compare your answers with a partner. How are your answers similar or different?

Mysterious Place or Creature	Question
The Great Pyramid	*Why did the Egyptians build this pyramid?*
Sphinx	*How do some archaeologists believe the Sphinx was damaged?*
Machu Picchu	
Stonehenge	
Easter Island	
Loch Ness monster	
Bigfoot and Yeti	

Work with a partner. Take turns asking and answering your questions.

100

EXTENSION

Copy the chart into your notebook. Choose one of the mysteries from "Fact or Fiction?" In the first column, write your topic and what you already know about it. In the second column, write a question you have about your topic. Then look for the answer to your question in an encyclopedia or other book, or on the Internet. Then write what you learned and how you learned it.

What I Know	What I Would Like to Know	What I Learned	How I Learned It

DISCUSSION

Discuss in pairs or small groups.

1. What do some people believe the Loch Ness monster is? What do you think it is? Why?

2. Which mystery do you think is the most interesting? Why?

3. What other mysteries do you know about? (For example, think about a mystery someone told you, you read about, or you saw in a movie.)

4. Imagine that a city in the United States was abandoned today, and archaeologists rediscovered it 100 years in the future. What clues might help them understand how people live today?

5. Do you think there are creatures in the world today that are unknown to science? Why or why not?

*In each of these three stories, the characters tell only part of the **truth**. As you read, try to figure out what the characters do not say. What is the whole truth? What are **lies**? Each story ends with a question. If you can't answer it, reread the story and look at the pictures to find the information you need.*

Truth or Lies?

George Shannon

Stolen Rope

A man in Trinidad was being led through town on his way to jail. His hands were chained behind his back, and one of his ankles was chained to the officer who was leading him. As the two men neared the **village square**, a former neighbor of the arrested man passed by.

---

truth, what is true; the correct facts
lies, things that are not true
village square, central part of a village

"What have you done that you're in chains and sentenced to jail?"

The chained man sighed. "I picked up a rope I found on the ground."

"You poor man!" said the neighbor. "There's more **injustice** in the **courts** than I realized."

"I know. It's terrible. Please tell them to set me free."

The man being taken to jail had spoken the truth, but he was also far from **innocent**.

What is the truth, the whole truth? And where's the lie?

The Whole Truth ———————
While it was true that the thief was being **punished** for picking up a rope, he was lying by what he did *not* say. The rope he picked up was tied to a cow.

---

injustice, unfairness
courts, places where someone is asked about a crime
innocent, not guilty of doing something wrong
punished, made to suffer because of doing something
  wrong

The Cookie Jar

Helen's mother had finished baking a **batch** of cookies when a neighbor came over and asked for help.

"I'll just be gone a few minutes," said her mother as she put the cookies into the cookie jar. "No snacking while I'm next door. These are for the party tonight."

When Helen's mother returned and checked the cookie jar, there was only one cookie left.

"Helen!" she called as she stomped upstairs. "I told you *not* to eat those cookies I made for the party tonight."

"I didn't touch one," said Helen.

"Well, they sure didn't fly away **on their own**! You can stay in your room till you decide to tell the truth."

What is the truth, the whole truth?
And where's the lie?

The Whole Truth

Helen's exact words, "I didn't touch one," were true. She had not touched *one* cookie, the only one she'd left in the jar uneaten. She had, however, touched—and eaten—all the rest.

---

batch, group of things
on their own, by themselves

BEFORE YOU GO ON . . .

1. What reason did the man from Trinidad give for going to jail? Why was he really going to jail?

2. What did Helen tell her mother? Did she tell the truth?

HOW ABOUT YOU?

- Do you think the man from Trinidad and Helen deserved to be punished?

School Days

A boy came running into the house for a snack after school and gave his mother a hug.

"How was your day?" asked his mother.

The boy grinned. "I got **a hundred** on my math and history tests!"

"That's wonderful," said his mother. "We'll celebrate with a special supper tonight."

It was a delicious meal, but when **report cards** came the next week, the boy's mother discovered there had been nothing to celebrate after all.

"How could you get an F in history and a D in math when you didn't miss anything on your tests last week? Did they catch you **cheating**? I certainly hope you weren't telling me lies!"

"Oh, no," answered the boy. "I'd never cheat. And as sure as I didn't cheat, I told you the truth."

His mother **grumbled** and frowned. "Well, something's not what it seems to be. I'm sure of that."

What is the truth, the whole truth?
And where's the lie?

The Whole Truth ———————————

The boy had gotten a hundred on his math and history tests. But it was a **combined score** of 100 for both tests—a 60 on the math test and a 40 on the history test.

---

a hundred, 100—a perfect score
report cards, documents giving a student's grades
cheating, doing something that is not honest
grumbled, complained in a quiet but angry way
combined score, total amount

BEFORE YOU GO ON . . .

1. What score did the boy say he got on his math and history tests?
2. What grades did he get on his report card?

HOW ABOUT YOU?

- Why do you think the boy lied about his grades?

Link the Readings

Think about the text "Fact or Fiction?" and reread "Truth or Lies?" Then copy the chart into your notebook and complete it. Compare your charts in small groups.

Title of Selection	Type of Text (Genre)	Fiction or Nonfiction	Purpose of Selection	Mystery I Liked Best
"Fact or Fiction?"	informational text		to inform and entertain	
"Truth or Lies?"		fiction		

DISCUSSION

Discuss in pairs or small groups.

1. Look at the chart you made. What two mysteries did you like best? Why?

2. Some mysteries in "Fact or Fiction?" might never be solved. Others might be solved. Choose one mystery that you think might or might not be solved and explain your answer.

3. In "Truth or Lies?" each character tells a half-truth. Find this sentence and discuss why it tells only part of the truth.

4. Imagine you are a group of archaeologists. You must choose a mysterious historical site to study. Which place will you choose? Why?

Connect to Writing

GRAMMAR

The Present Progressive

The **present progressive** describes an action that is happening now. The present progressive uses a form of *be* with a verb + *-ing*.

I **am looking** at a pyramid.	*They* **are visiting** the ancient city.
He **is taking** a picture.	*We* **are swimming** in the lake.
She **is eating** a cookie.	*You* **are telling** the truth.
It **is raining** today.	

Note: When the verb ends in *-e*, drop the *-e* before adding *-ing*.

tak**e**	tak**ing**

Some verbs double the final consonant before adding *-ing*.

swi**m**	swim**ming**

Practice

Look at the picture. In your notebook, write sentences about what the people are doing. Use the present progressive. Here are some phrases to help you.

take a picture	move a stone	visit an ancient city
eat a cookie	drink water	read a map

Example: *A man is taking a picture.*

106

SKILLS FOR WRITING

Using Prepositional Phrases

Some **prepositions** show place—where people or things are located. A **prepositional phrase** is a preposition + a noun or pronoun. You can use prepositional phrases to tell where people or things are.

Prepositions	Prepositional Phrases
under	The dog is **under** the table.
behind	The cow is **behind** it.
next to	The statue is **next to** the cookie jar.
in	The cookies are **in** it.
between	The sun is **between** the pyramids.
near	The man is **near** them.
on	The apples are **on** the plate.

Read this paragraph about the picture on page 106. Then answer the question.

Natalia Dare

At the Pyramids

There are people and animals from all over the world visiting the pyramids. A girl is digging in the sand, a dog is running with a bone in its mouth, and a stork is carrying a baby with its beak. A girl is reading a map, a camel is bathing in a tub, a woman is looking at a bone lying on the sand, and a man is standing behind a palm tree. A man with a surfboard is running, a snake is coming out of a basket in front of a tent called the Sands Hotel, and a camel is wearing sunglasses.

Describe what other people and animals are doing in the picture. Use prepositional phrases and the present progressive.

WRITING ASSIGNMENT

Descriptive Paragraph

You will write a description of the picture below, using the present progressive and prepositional phrases.

1. Read Reread the paragraph on page 107. How do the prepositional phrases help the reader visualize the people and things in the picture?

Writing Strategy: Asking Questions

Before you describe a picture, ask yourself questions about what you see. The writer of "At the Pyramids" asked herself these questions before writing her description.

- *Who is in the picture?*
- *Where are they?*
- *What are they doing?*

Answer these questions when you plan your description.

---

2. Write Write a description of the picture, using the answers to your questions. Use prepositional phrases and the present progressive.

EDITING CHECKLIST

Did you . . .

▶ include prepositional phrases?

▶ use the present progressive correctly?

▶ indent the first sentence in the paragraph?

▶ start each sentence with a capital letter?

▶ end each sentence with a period?

Check Your Knowledge

Language Development

1. What is the difference between a fact and an opinion? Give an example of each.

2. What is a mystery? What do mystery writers do to help readers solve a mystery story?

3. Give examples of three sentences using the present progressive.

4. What do prepositional phrases tell us? Give examples.

Academic Content

1. What new science and social studies vocabulary did you learn in Part 1? What do the words mean?

2. What does an archaeologist do?

3. What is mysterious about the three Pyramids of Giza?

4. What are two mysteries about Easter Island?

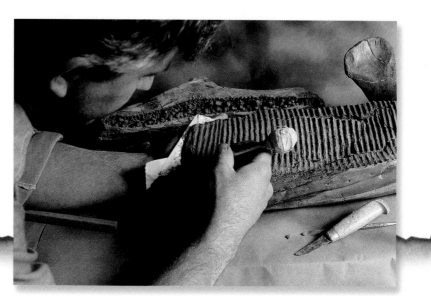

▲ An archaeologist works on a dinosaur's jaw.

Prepare to Read

OBJECTIVES

LANGUAGE DEVELOPMENT

Reading:
- Vocabulary building: *Context, dictionary skills*
- Reading strategy: *Compare and contrast*
- Text types: *Mysteries, instructions*
- Literary elements: *Suspense, plot*

Writing:
- Writing strategy: *Flowchart*
- Treasure hunt clues
- Science experiment steps
- Punctuation and capitalization

Listening/Speaking:
- Instructions for science experiments
- Read instructions to an audience
- Support spoken ideas with evidence

Grammar:
- Imperative sentences

Viewing/Representing:
- Diagrams in science experiments

ACADEMIC CONTENT
- Science vocabulary
- Draw conclusions
- Follow steps of science experiments

BACKGROUND

Teenage Detectives includes three short mystery stories. A mystery story contains a problem that has to be solved. The main character or characters gather clues to solve the case. In these stories, the two teenage detectives like to solve mysteries in their neighborhood.

A detective is someone who tries to solve mysteries. For example, a detective tries to find out who has committed a crime. A detective is usually good at asking questions.

Make connections Detectives use special tools to help them with their job. Look at the picture. How do you think the detectives might use these tools?

LEARN KEY WORDS

case
evidence
guilty
phony
solution
up to mischief

VOCABULARY

Read these sentences. Use the context to figure out the meaning of the **red** words. Use a dictionary to check your answers. Write each word and its meaning in your notebook.

1. The detective solved the **case** of the stolen treasure.
2. He looked for **evidence**, such as fingerprints, to find the thief.
3. The thief was **guilty** of the crime, and the judge sent him to jail.
4. The "doctor" was a **phony**! She'd never gone to medical school!
5. We had all the information, so the **solution** to the problem was not difficult.
6. The boys are always **up to mischief**, so they are often punished.

READING STRATEGY

Using a Graphic Organizer to Compare and Contrast

When you **compare**, you find similarities—things that are the same. When you **contrast**, you find differences—things that are different.

Good readers write notes in a chart (such as a Venn diagram) when they need to compare and contrast two or more texts, or something within a text, such as characters. Charts and Venn diagrams help readers to see and remember information. Try using a graphic organizer to compare and contrast the main characters, the settings, the crimes, and the criminals.

"The Case of the Surprise Visitor"

money stolen

Both stories

mystery

"The Case of the Defaced Sidewalk"

sidewalk defaced

Mystery Stories

As you read the three mystery stories, think about how the stories, the characters, and the settings are similar or different.

Teenage Detectives

Teenage cousins Max and Nina love solving crimes in their town, Harborville. See if you can find the solutions to the following mysterious cases.

The Case of the Surprise Visitor

Carol Farley

The clock in the courthouse ahead of Max showed six o'clock. As it began **chiming**, he noticed a tall man with a **briefcase** walking toward him. The man turned around, looked at the clock, and then quickened his steps. He took an envelope out of his briefcase, dropped it in a mailbox, and continued on his way. Max moved faster, too. Miss Fritz, Harborville's oldest music teacher, had invited him for dinner. He didn't want to be late.

"I'm glad you could come," Miss Fritz said. "I've made a lovely salad for us." She **gestured** Max to a chair. "Good thing I prepared ahead. A **surprise** visitor just left."

"Who visited?" Max asked.

"A teacher from Harborville's School for the Deaf. He was totally **deaf** himself, poor man, but he could **read lips** perfectly. He had the loveliest **penmanship** when he wanted to tell me something."

"Why was he here?" Max asked.

chiming, making a sound like a bell
briefcase, case for carrying papers or books
gestured, used hands to tell something
surprise, unexpected
deaf, hearing impaired
read lips, understand a speaker by looking at his or her lips
penmanship, handwriting

"Well, evidently the school **is low on funds**. I was glad to help out. I had just cashed my social security check so I was able to give him five hundred dollars."

"Did he just leave? Was he a tall man with a briefcase?"

"Yes."

"We'd better phone the police. I think that man was a phony. I know for sure he wasn't totally deaf."

How did Max figure it out? ————

The clock was behind the man as he was walking, so he could not have seen it. He turned around at the sound of the chimes, so he obviously heard them and therefore was not deaf.

"You didn't waste time solving this case," Nina told Max later.

"Just watch me solve another one soon," Max answered.

is low on funds, doesn't have much money

The Case of the Defaced Sidewalk

Carol Farley

One Saturday morning, Nina saw the **three musketeers** in the mall. Jenny, Brittany, and Mitzi called themselves the three musketeers because they were always together.

"I've been shopping for **sandals**," Jenny told Nina. "But I have such a wide foot nothing seems to fit. We've been looking everywhere."

"And it's been slow going," Mitzi added. "On account of Brittany's—"

"I know," Nina said, looking at Brittany. "I heard you **sprained** your ankle in gym yesterday. Does it still hurt a lot?"

"It's okay as long as I move really slowly," Brittany told her. "We're going to get ice cream at the Just Desserts Shop now. Want to join us?"

"Better not. Max is meeting me at home. See you later."

Nina was **taking a shortcut** through Harborville's city park when she saw Mr. Hansen kneeling beside a new sidewalk. The **city maintenance man** frowned as she drew closer.

"Somebody jumped right in the middle here while the cement was still wet," he said, pointing at two narrow footprints

embedded in the concrete. "Now I'll have to rip out this section and redo it. I sure can't leave the sidewalk looking like this!"

"Any idea of who did it?" Nina asked.

"A kid over there on the slide said that three girls named Brittany, Mitzi, and Jenny were the only ones near here. But he doesn't know which one ruined my sidewalk."

"I know who did it," Nina declared.

How did Nina figure it out? ————

The footprints were narrow. Jenny has wide feet. Brittany couldn't have jumped because of her sprained ankle. So Mitzi had to be the guilty one.

"You were able to walk into a quick solution for this case," Max told Nina later. "I sure am glad that I'm on your side."

"I had concrete evidence," Nina answered.

---

defaced, damaged
Three Musketeers, a book about three characters who
    share adventures
sandals, open shoes worn in warm weather
sprained, hurt but didn't break
taking a shortcut, going a faster way
city maintenance man, man who fixes and cleans
    things for a city

The Case of the Disappearing Signs

Elizabeth Dearl

Nina was eating cold pizza for lunch at Max's house one hot July day. Max's mom, Mrs. Decker, a **real-estate agent**, came in looking warm and weary.

"I'm so **disgusted**," she said. "Remember that old house over on Norton Drive that I **listed**? I put a FOR SALE sign up in the yard early this morning. I just drove by now and it's gone. This is the third sign this month that has disappeared."

"Why would anyone steal a **realtor's signs**?" Nina asked. "What would anybody do with them?"

---

real-estate agent, someone who sells houses
disgusted, upset or angry
listed, advertised; put on a list of items for sale
realtor's signs, signs that advertise a house

"Who knows?" Mrs. Decker poured herself a glass of lemonade. "Probably some kids with nothing better to do. I suppose they could use the signs to build something. They were the wooden ones."

Max nudged Nina. "Want to bike over and see what we can find out?"

"Not much there to see," his mother told him. "Only two houses on that whole street. An old lady—Mrs. Stearns—lives in the house next to the empty one."

"Maybe she saw something," Nina said. "Let's go ask."

Half an hour later, the two were biking toward the end of Norton Drive. A pick-up truck was parked in front of the empty house. A man was standing on the sidewalk looking in all directions.

"Do you kids know anything about this place?" he asked. "I'm from out of town, and my nephew, Paul, has been checking houses for me this past month. He thought I might like the one at the end of Norton Drive, so he let me borrow his truck to drive over here. But I don't know if this is the house he meant. There aren't any signs."

BEFORE YOU GO ON . . .

1 In "The Case of the Defaced Sidewalk," why is Mr. Hansen frowning?

2 In "The Case of the Disappearing Signs," who does Mrs. Decker think stole the signs?

HOW ABOUT YOU?

• Why do you think someone might steal a FOR SALE sign?

"This house is for sale," Max told him. "My mom is the real-estate agent."

"Great! Then can you tell me her name and company? I'd like to ask about this property. Paul tells me that houses in this part of town sell fast. He says this one has been **on the market** for quite some time. I'm glad I got here before it was sold! I just couldn't get over here any sooner."

As soon as Max gave him the information, the man drove off.

Nina stared after the truck. "Know what? His nephew, Paul, might have taken the signs. Maybe he didn't want people to see that the house was for sale until his uncle had a chance to look at it. You can put lots of things in the back of a truck."

Max nodded. "Let's ask Mrs. Stearns if she saw anything this morning."

Mrs. Stearns came to the door as soon as they knocked. She was gray-haired, but she stood straight and tall. "Oh, I think I

---

on the market, for sale

know who might have taken those signs," she told them. "Freddie Swanson. He lives a block away, and he's always up to mischief."

She held the door open as she talked, and Nina peeked inside. She liked the **cozy** living room. The sofa and chairs were velvet-covered **antiques**. Lace doilies covered the end tables. A large painting hung over the intricately carved fireplace mantel, and a cheerful fire **crackled** below.

"I know Freddie," Max said. "And I know where he lives. Let's go see him."

Freddie was putting a lawn mower in the garage when they reached his house. He **mopped his brow** as he talked to them. "Why would I take a dumb old sign?" he asked. "Besides, I've been out here doing yard work all morning."

Nina stared past him at the garage. Her parents could hardly get their car in her garage at home because of all the stuff in it, but this one was **practically bare**. Then she noticed a **crudely built** tree house in the yard. The boards were gray and weather-beaten.

She and Max talked as they biked back to his house. Mrs. Decker was washing the lunch dishes when they ran into the house.

"We think we know who took the signs," Nina told her.

---

cozy, comfortable
antiques, very old, valuable objects
crackled, made popping sounds
mopped his brow, wiped his forehead
practically bare, nearly empty
crudely built, not carefully made

116

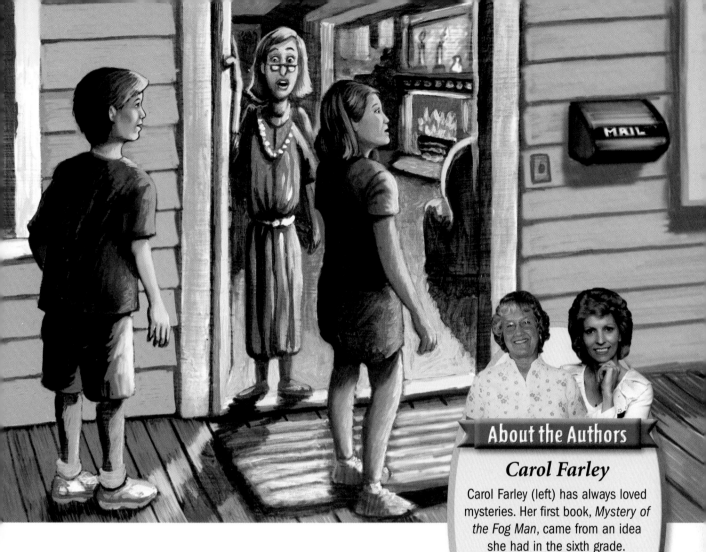

About the Authors

Carol Farley

Carol Farley (left) has always loved mysteries. Her first book, *Mystery of the Fog Man*, came from an idea she had in the sixth grade.

Elizabeth Dearl

Elizabeth Dearl (right) is a former Texas police officer. She is the author of several mystery novels.

How did Nina and Max figure it out?

There was no evidence to show that Paul had used his truck to transport the signs. The boards in Freddie's tree house were too old and worn to have been made with the signs. Mrs. Stearns had a fire in her fireplace on a hot July day. She didn't want neighbors moving in next door, so she took the signs and burned them in her fireplace so nobody would know the house was for sale.

"That fire was a **hot tip**," Nina said later as she joined Max and Mrs. Decker for a cold drink of lemonade.

---

hot tip, good clue

BEFORE YOU GO ON . . .

1. Why does Nina think the man's nephew, Paul, might have stolen the signs?

2. What does Mrs. Stearns say to suggest that Freddie stole the signs?

HOW ABOUT YOU?

- Did you guess who stole the signs?

117

Review and Practice

The three mystery stories that you read are similar in some ways and different in other ways. Reread the stories. Copy the chart into your notebook. Then complete the chart. Work in small groups. Use your charts to discuss similarities and differences in the three cases.

	Main Characters	Setting	Criminal	Description of the Crime
"The Case of the Surprise Visitor"			tall man with a briefcase	
"The Case of the Defaced Sidewalk"				Someone jumped into the wet cement in the sidewalk.
"The Case of the Disappearing Signs"	Max, Nina, Mrs. Decker			

Work in pairs. Copy the following story into your notebook. Choose your own words to fill in the blanks. Finish the story in your own words. Make it as funny as you can.

When we went into the school cafeteria, the cook said, "All the _____ and _____ from my kitchen disappeared last night. They were on this counter. How did it happen? There were no broken windows, and the door was locked."

Just then the cook's _____ dog ran toward us, jumping and barking.

"Outside, _____ !" the cook shouted.

We noticed that the dog had a _____ in its mouth.

We left the cafeteria and went to _____. Two students in our class, _____ and _____, were sitting on a _____ eating _____ .

"Where did you get those?" we asked.

_____

_____

Work with another pair of students. Take turns reading your mystery stories aloud. Can you guess each other's solutions to the mystery? How are your mysteries similar? How are they different?

Discuss in pairs or small groups.

1. What clue helped Nina figure out that Mrs. Stearns took the signs? What do you think about what Mrs. Stearns did?

2. Think of words to describe Max and Nina. How are they similar? Are you like Max and Nina in any way? If so, how?

3. Which of the three cases was the easiest to solve? Why?

Science

*Read the descriptions of two science experiments. Look at how the **materials** and the **method** are organized.*

How To Make a Friend Disappear

Materials
- two chairs
- a small mirror

Method

1. Sit on a chair with a wall to your right. Ask your partner to sit **opposite** you (see the diagram). Your partner should sit very **still**.

2. Hold the bottom of the mirror with your left hand. Put the edge of the mirror against the side of your nose or slightly in front of it. The **reflecting surface** should face the wall. Don't move your head.

3. Turn the mirror so that your right eye sees only the reflection of the wall. Your left eye should look straight ahead at your partner.

4. Move your right hand in front of the wall like you are **erasing** a chalkboard. Watch as parts of your friend's face disappear!

Magicians use this trick to make objects "disappear." They use mirrors to hide the objects from view.

Some people see this effect more easily than others. A few people never see it. You may have to try it several times. Don't **give up**!

---

give up, stop trying

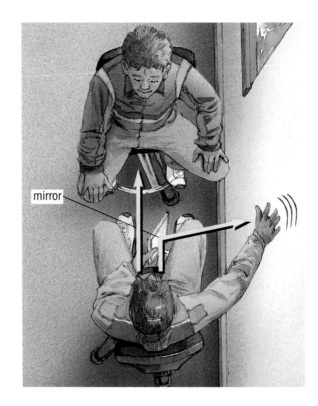

mirror

---

materials, things you need
method, instructions; way to do something
opposite, facing; across from
still, without moving
reflecting surface, side of the mirror where you can see yourself
erasing, removing something

If you don't see your friend's face disappear, one of your eyes might be stronger than the other. Try the experiment again. This time, change the eye you use to look at the person and the eye you use to look at the wall.

Why Is It So?

Usually, your two eyes see slightly different pictures of the world around you. Your brain combines these two pictures to create a single image.

In this experiment, the mirror lets your eyes see two very different views. One eye looks straight ahead at your partner, while the other eye looks at the wall and your moving hand. Your brain tries to put together a picture that makes sense by choosing parts of both views.

Young Girl or Old Woman?

Your brain works hard to understand the images that you see in the world around you, based on your experiences. Which do you see first—a young girl or an old woman? Once you can see both, your brain can easily switch between one and the other.

BEFORE YOU GO ON . . .

1 What did you need to do this experiment?

2 What new information did you learn about your brain?

HOW ABOUT YOU?
- Did the experiment work easily for you?

WATER TRICK

Materials

- a drinking glass
- a **handkerchief**
- a rubber band

Method

1. Fill a glass three-quarters full with water.
2. Place a **damp** handkerchief over the top of the glass.
3. Place a rubber band around the rim of the glass so that it is holding the handkerchief.
4. Push down on the center of the handkerchief until it touches the water. Make sure the rubber band stays around the glass.
5. Keep your fingers pressed on the handkerchief and turn the glass upside down.
6. Pull the handkerchief tight, still keeping the rubber band on, so that the curved shape disappears. The water will remain in the glass.

---

handkerchief, square piece of cloth
damp, a bit wet

Why Is It So?

Molecules at the surface of water attract each other and **clump together**. This is called surface tension. Surface tension prevents the molecules from passing through the small holes of the handkerchief.

At home you can look at different liquids and see how much or how little surface tension they have. Put a drop of water onto a plate and it will form a rounded ball. This is because of surface tension. Put a drop of vinegar onto a plate. Put a drop of oil on a different plate. Can you tell which liquid has more surface tension?

---

molecules, the smallest part into which a substance can be divided without changing its form
clump together, form a group or mass

BEFORE YOU GO ON . . .

1. List the three materials needed for this trick.
2. What prevents the water from going through the handkerchief?

HOW ABOUT YOU?

- Which of the two experiments did you find more interesting? Why?

Link the Readings

Review the mystery stories and reread the science experiments. Think about the two kinds of readings as you look at the chart. Then copy the chart into your notebook and complete it. Compare your answers in small groups.

Title of Selection	Type of Text (Genre)	Fiction or Nonfiction	Purpose of Selection	The Mystery
"The Case of the Surprise Visitor"	short story			
"The Case of the Defaced Sidewalk"		fiction		
"The Case of the Disappearing Signs"				
"How to Make a Friend Disappear"	informational text		to explain something about science	
"Water Trick"		nonfiction		Water remains in the glass.

DISCUSSION

Discuss in pairs or small groups.

1. How are the two science experiments similar to a mystery story? How are they different?
2. Would you prefer to be a detective or a scientist? Why?

Connect to Writing

GRAMMAR

Imperatives

An **imperative** gives an instruction, a direction, or an order. In sentences with an imperative, the subject is not stated, but it is understood to be *you*. Imperative sentences end with a period or an exclamation point.

SUBJECT	VERB
(You)	**Follow** the directions.
	Sit on a chair.
	Move your right hand.
	Fill the glass with water.
	Try the experiment again!

Practice

1. Find five imperative sentences in "How to Make a Friend Disappear" and "Water Trick." Write them in your notebook. Underline the imperative verb in each sentence.

2. Now work with a partner. Write five new imperative sentences that tell your partner what to do. Read your sentences to your partner and see if he or she can follow your instructions.

   Example: *Put your hand on your head.*

3. What are the imperative verbs in the cartoon?

PEANUTS reprinted by permission of United Feature Syndicate, Inc.

SKILLS FOR WRITING

Writing Clues

A treasure hunt is a game. In a treasure hunt, you get clues, which are directions you follow to find a hidden treasure or prize. Read these clues. Then answer the questions.

> Jason Preston
>
> Treasure Hunt Clues
>
> Start at the big car.
>
> Walk ten steps between two large trees.
>
> Go into the yellow house.
>
> Walk down the hall.
>
> Turn right and go into the bedroom.
>
> Turn left and walk to the desk.
>
> Look under the desk.
>
> Pick up the box.
>
> Open the box!

1. What verbs are used?
2. What kinds of sentences are used to give the clue
3. What punctuation marks are used at the end of tl sentences?

WRITING ASSIGNMENT

Clues for a Treasure Hunt

You will write clues for a treasure hunt in your school.

1. **Read** Reread the clues on page 125. Are the clues easy to understand?

Writing Strategy: Flowchart

A flowchart helps you organize your clues in order. Decide where you want your treasure hunt to begin and write the place in the first box. Decide where you want your treasure hunt to end and write the place in the last box. Then fill in the other boxes. Write clues that tell how to get from the start to the finish. Look at this example:

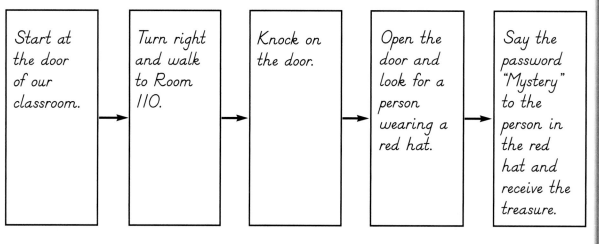

| Start at the door of our classroom. | Turn right and walk to Room 110. | Knock on the door. | Open the door and look for a person wearing a red hat. | Say the password "Mystery" to the person in the red hat and receive the treasure. |

2. **Make a flowchart** Think of a treasure for your classmates to look for. Then make a flowchart in your notebook, listing each clue.

3. **Write** Write the clues for your treasure hunt. Use imperatives. After your classmates find your treasure, talk about your clues. Are there ways to make the clues easier to understand?

EDITING CHECKLIST

Did you . . .

▶ write clues that are easy to understand?

▶ use imperatives?

▶ use a capital letter at the beginning of each clue?

▶ use a period or exclamation point at the end of each clue?

Check Your Knowledge

Language Development

1. What do you do when you compare and contrast texts?
2. What is suspense? Give an example.
3. What is a plot?
4. What is the purpose of a mystery story?
5. Use the term *up to mischief* in a sentence.
6. Give an example of an imperative. When do you use imperatives?
7. Who is usually the subject in an imperative sentence?
8. Describe a flowchart. When do you use one?

Academic Content

1. What new science vocabulary did you learn in Part 2? What do the words mean?
2. When you look at something, your eyes see different images. What part of the body combines these images into one image?
3. What is a treasure hunt?

Put It All Together

OBJECTIVES

Integrate Skills
- Listening/
  Speaking:
  *Instructions to
  solve a
  problem*
- Writing:
  *Instructions
  for a science
  experiment*

**Investigate
Themes**
- Projects
- Further
  reading

INSTRUCTIONS TO SOLVE A PROBLEM

You will give instructions on how to solve a problem.

1 **Think about it** Ask yourself: What problems do I have to solve at school? For example, how can I find a book in the library or information on the Internet? Make a list.

Work with two or three classmates. Compare your lists of problems. Then choose one problem that you think most people in your class have. Brainstorm solutions to the problem. Then choose the best solution.

2 **Organize** Work together to write the steps to solve the problem. Make a flowchart to show the steps. Make sure your steps are in the correct order. Use imperative sentences.

3 **Practice** Choose one group member to be your speaker. Have the speaker practice reading the steps to your solution. Other group members can suggest changes to improve the instructions.

SPEAKING TIPS

- Present each step clearly.
- Pause a few seconds after each step.
- Ask listeners if they have any questions.

4 **Present and evaluate** Have your speaker present your problem and solution to the class. Other group members can help the speaker—for example, by showing the flowchart.

After each speaker finishes, evaluate the presentation. Were the steps clear and easy to understand? What did you like best about the presentation? Do you have suggestions for improvement?

LISTENING TIPS

- If you can't hear the speaker, you may say, "Excuse me, could you speak louder, please?"
- If there is something you don't understand, you may say, "Could you please repeat that point?"

INSTRUCTIONS FOR A SCIENCE EXPERIMENT

When writing instructions for a science experiment, it is very important to write the steps in the correct order. The writer usually uses imperative sentences that are short and easy to understand.

Good instructions for a science experiment include the following characteristics:

- a list of materials used in the experiment
- clear, simple language to describe the steps
- a correct sequence of steps
- a concluding step that explains what happens in the experiment

You will write instructions for a science experiment. Use the following steps, the model on page 130, and the pictures to help you.

 Prewrite Look at the four pictures of the science experiment on page 131. List the materials that you need to do the experiment.

Study each picture. Make a flowchart to describe what happens in each picture. Use the words in the box under the pictures to complete the flowchart.

WRITING TIPS

- Remember to use imperative sentences to write instructions.
- Use prepositional phrases in the instructions to describe where things are located.
- A science experiment must be done in the correct sequence. Number each step so that the order of your instructions is clear and correct.

Before you write a first draft of your instructions, read the following model for another experiment. Note the characteristics of clear instructions.

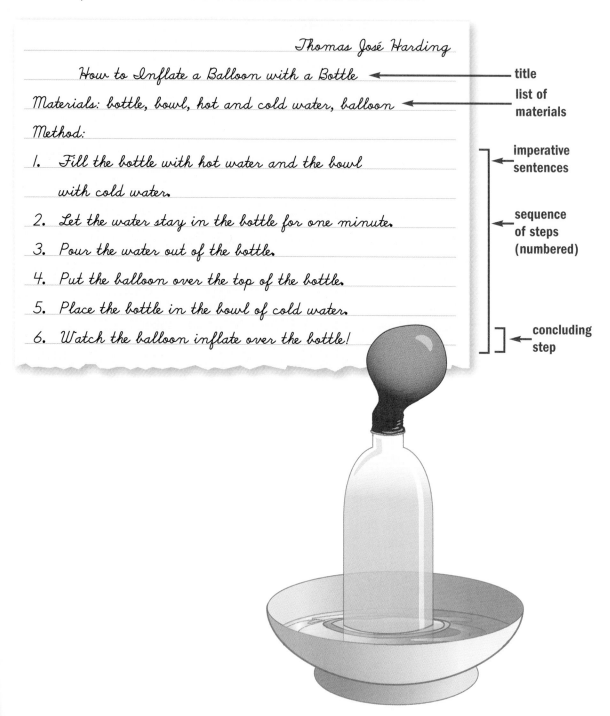

Thomas José Harding

How to Inflate a Balloon with a Bottle ← **title**

Materials: bottle, bowl, hot and cold water, balloon ← **list of materials**

Method:

1. Fill the bottle with hot water and the bowl with cold water.

2. Let the water stay in the bottle for one minute.

3. Pour the water out of the bottle.

4. Put the balloon over the top of the bottle.

5. Place the bottle in the bowl of cold water.

6. Watch the balloon inflate over the bottle!

imperative sentences

sequence of steps (numbered)

concluding step

2 **Draft** Use the model and your flowchart to write your instructions for the following science experiment. Use the words in the box.

pour	glass	bottle	salt shaker	sink
salt	olive oil	water	shake	

3 **Edit** Work in pairs. Trade papers and read each other's instructions. Use the questions in the editing checklist to evaluate each other's work.

EDITING CHECKLIST

Did you . . .
- ▶ include a title and list of materials?
- ▶ write the steps in the correct order?
- ▶ use imperative sentences?
- ▶ use prepositional phrases?
- ▶ use correct punctuation?

4 **Revise** Revise your instructions. Add information and correct mistakes, if necessary.

5 **Publish** Share your experiment with your teacher and classmates. If possible, perform the experiment.

PROJECTS

Work in pairs or small groups. Choose one of these projects.

1 Create an interesting mystery story about Max and Nina. Give clues to your readers. Then read your story to the class.

2 Choose one of the mysterious places or creatures from "Fact or Fiction?" Draw a picture of the place or creature and write sentences that describe it. Read the description and let your classmates guess what you are describing. Show them the picture when they guess correctly.

3 Find simple science experiments on the Internet, in a textbook, or in a library book. Try one of these experiments at home with a family member and talk about what causes these scientific "mysteries" to happen. Share what you learn with the class.

4 Invite a police detective to your classroom to learn more about how crimes are solved. Prepare a list of questions about detective work before your speaker arrives. Ask the detective to share the tools he or she uses on the job. Also talk about special skills that a detective needs to have.

5 Perform one of the cases from *Teenage Detectives* in a readers theatre. Group members choose their roles. Choose a narrator—someone who tells the parts of the story that the characters don't speak. Practice saying your lines before you perform the story for your classmates. Then perform your scene for the class.

Further Reading

To find out more about the theme of this unit, choose from these reading suggestions.

Beastly Tales, Real Encounters with Mysterious Monsters, **Malcolm Yorke** All around the world people tell stories about seeing mysterious monsters. The storytellers are often accused of making things up. But sometimes a discovery is made that proves them right. Few people believed stories about a manlike ape in Africa, a dragon in Indonesia, or a huge sea monster with long tentacles. However, we now know these creatures really exist!

Rip Van Winkle and ***The Legend of Sleepy Hollow,*** **Washington Irving** One day Rip Van Winkle goes to the mountains with his dog. Who are the strange old men, and why are they there? In *The Legend of Sleepy Hollow*, Ichabod Crane is a teacher who likes ghost stories. Are there really ghosts at Sleepy Hollow, and will Ichabod see one of them?

The Mysterious Island, **Jules Verne** There are three men, a boy, and a dog in a balloon over the Pacific Ocean, but only two men and the boy arrive on the island. Mysterious things start happening. Are they the only people on the island? Where are the other man and his dog?

Detective Work, **John Escott** A diamond necklace is stolen from a museum. Everyone who works at the museum might be the thief. But who really took the necklace, and why? Paul, a young student, helps the police find the thief.

Call Me Consuelo, **Ofelia Dumas Lachtman** Twelve-year-old orphan Consuelo Harburton reluctantly leaves her Mexican-American aunt, uncle, and cousins to live with her American grandmother in Los Angeles. Consuelo struggles with the changes in her life, but she soon becomes involved with solving some mysterious robberies in her new neighborhood.

Conflict

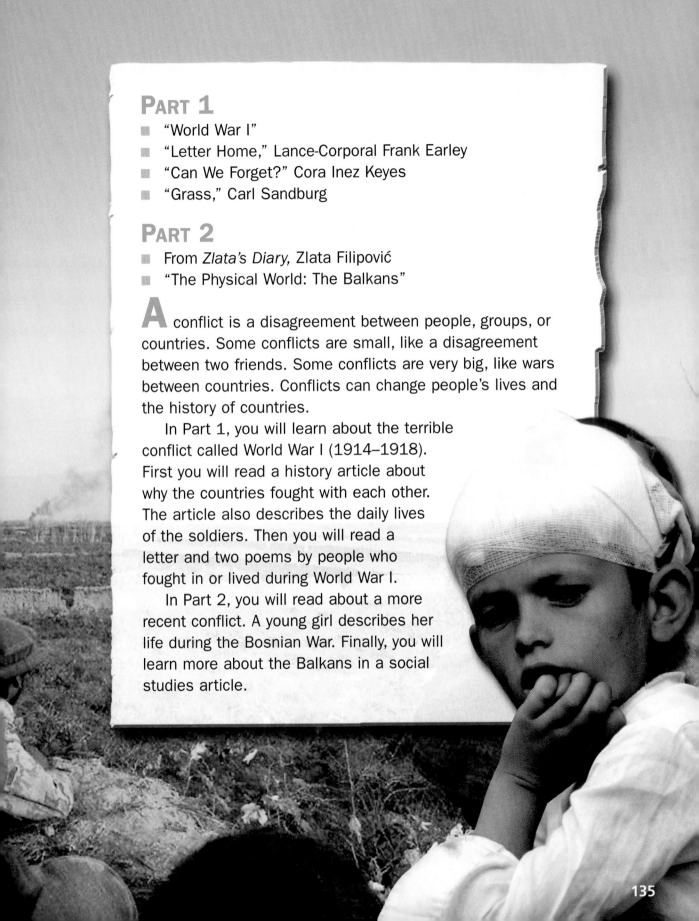

PART 1

- "World War I"
- "Letter Home," Lance-Corporal Frank Earley
- "Can We Forget?" Cora Inez Keyes
- "Grass," Carl Sandburg

PART 2

- From *Zlata's Diary,* Zlata Filipović
- "The Physical World: The Balkans"

A conflict is a disagreement between people, groups, or countries. Some conflicts are small, like a disagreement between two friends. Some conflicts are very big, like wars between countries. Conflicts can change people's lives and the history of countries.

In Part 1, you will learn about the terrible conflict called World War I (1914–1918). First you will read a history article about why the countries fought with each other. The article also describes the daily lives of the soldiers. Then you will read a letter and two poems by people who fought in or lived during World War I.

In Part 2, you will read about a more recent conflict. A young girl describes her life during the Bosnian War. Finally, you will learn more about the Balkans in a social studies article.

135

Prepare to Read

OBJECTIVES

LANGUAGE DEVELOPMENT

Reading:
- Vocabulary building: *Context, dictionary skills*
- Reading strategy: *Noting causes and effects*
- Text types: *Social studies article, letter, poems*
- Literary element: *Rhyme*

Writing:
- Cause-and-effect organization
- Cause-and-effect paragraph
- Editing checklist

Listening/Speaking:
- For enjoyment
- Intonation patterns
- Analysis of oral interpretation

Grammar:
- Conjunction *so*

Viewing/Representing:
- Timeline, maps, painting

ACADEMIC CONTENT
- History vocabulary
- Causes and effects of World War I

BACKGROUND

"World War I" is an informational history text. It is nonfiction, which means that it is about real facts and events.

Make connections Work in pairs. Study the map and timeline of World War I and answer the questions.

▲ Europe before World War I

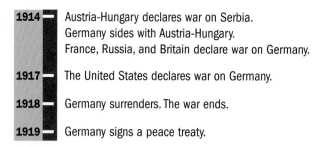

1914 — Austria-Hungary declares war on Serbia.
Germany sides with Austria-Hungary.
France, Russia, and Britain declare war on Germany.

1917 — The United States declares war on Germany.

1918 — Germany surrenders. The war ends.

1919 — Germany signs a peace treaty.

1. When did World War I begin?
2. When did the United States enter the war?
3. How many years did the war last?

LEARN KEY WORDS

allies
enemy
surrendered
tension
terrorists
treaty

VOCABULARY

Read these sentences. Use the context to figure out the meaning of the **red** words. Use a dictionary to check your answers. Write each word and its meaning in your notebook.

1. Britain and France were **allies**, so they fought together against other countries.
2. Britain and France's **enemy** was Germany.
3. Germany knew it could not win the war, so it **surrendered**.
4. The **tension** between the two countries grew into a conflict.
5. A group of **terrorists** hid bombs in the train, frightening the passengers.
6. A **treaty** was signed in 1919, and peace returned to Europe.

READING STRATEGY

Noting Causes and Effects

History texts often have **cause-and-effect organization**. A **cause** is a person, event, or thing that makes something happen. The thing that happens is the **effect**. In a text that has cause-and-effect organization, the writer discusses causes and then shows their effects.

As you read, follow these steps:

- Look for words that show effect, for example, *so:*

  cause   effect
  *The two countries couldn't agree, **so** there was a lot of tension.*

- Look for words that show cause, for example, *because:*

  effect   cause
  *Many people lost their homes **because** the city was bombed.*

Note that sometimes the effect is stated before the cause. Copy the chart into your notebook. Use it to note causes and effects.

Cause	⟶	Effect
	⟶	

Social Studies

First, preview the article. Then, as you read each paragraph more carefully, look for words such as so *and* because *to find causes and effects. Use the cause-and-effect chart you copied from page 137.*

World War I

Background to the Conflict

At the beginning of the twentieth century, there was a lot of tension among countries in Europe. One reason was the balance of power—that is, no one country wanted another country to have more power than it did. Britain, France, and Germany were competing with each other for **overseas trade**. Britain was worried because Germany had bigger, more modern factories. Germany was worried because France had a lot of power and wealth and **colonies** in Africa. Germany wanted more land and **resources**. Also, Russia and Austria-Hungary were trying to gain more power in the Balkan states in southeast Europe. Because of this tension, the countries formed two powerful **alliances**:

▲ A German factory in 1914

- Britain, France, Russia
- Germany, Austria-Hungary, Italy

By the middle of 1914, Europe was close to war.

---

overseas trade, the buying and selling of foreign products
colonies, countries or areas that are ruled by other countries
resources, things that create wealth, such as land and energy
alliances, agreements between countries to become allies

138

◀ Bosnian student Gavrilo Princip fired the fatal shot.

▲ Archduke Ferdinand and his wife shortly before the assassination

The Assassination

In 1914, Austria-Hungary ruled Bosnia, a small state in the Balkans in eastern Europe. Some people in Serbia, another state in the Balkans, wanted Bosnia to be part of Serbia because many Serbs lived in Bosnia. They wanted to be independent of Austria-Hungary.

Archduke Franz Ferdinand, the son of the **emperor** of Austria-Hungary, visited Sarajevo, the capital of Bosnia. The Serbs in Bosnia were unhappy about the archduke's visit. On June 28, 1914, a Bosnian student, supported by a group of Serbian terrorists, assassinated him. Austria-Hungary declared war on Serbia on July 28. The war quickly spread as other countries defended their allies. By mid-August 1914, most of Europe was at war.

---

assassination, the killing of an important person
emperor, ruler of a country or countries

BEFORE YOU GO ON . . .

1 Who ruled Bosnia in 1914? Why did this cause tension?

2 What happened as a result of Archduke Ferdinand's assassination?

HOW ABOUT YOU?

• Do you know about any other assassinations? Discuss.

The War Grows

Within a year, many countries had joined in the war. This chart shows how the countries were divided.

Allied Nations ("The Allies")		Central Powers (Fighting against the Allies)
Britain	Australia	Germany
France	New Zealand	Austria-Hungary
Russia	Canada	Bulgaria
Belgium	South Africa	Ottoman Empire (Turkey, etc.)
Portugal	Soldiers from	Italy (changed sides and joined
Greece	French and	the Allies in 1915)
Serbia	British colonies	
Montenegro	in Africa, Asia,	
Romania	the Pacific, and	
	the Caribbean	

The "First Modern War"

World War I is often called the "first modern war" because soldiers used modern weapons for the first time. New **inventions** were created using the latest **technology**. Some new weapons used during World War I were:

Machine guns   These guns, invented by an American, shot many bullets very quickly.

Submarines   These underwater ships shot torpedoes—bombs that are fired underwater.

Poison gas and gas masks   Poison gas caused **choking**, blindness, **blisters**, and sometimes death. Gas masks protected soldiers.

Tanks   These heavy vehicles had big guns and metal belts over their wheels, so they were difficult to attack and destroy.

Periscope rifles   Two mirrors were attached to a rifle, so that when lifted over the top of the trenches, the soldier could see the enemy.

Fighter airplanes   These small planes were armed with machine guns.

---

inventions, completely new things
technology, the knowledge and equipment that is used in the making of machines, etc.
choking, coughing; gasping for breath
blisters, lumps on the skin, filled with liquid, usually caused by burning

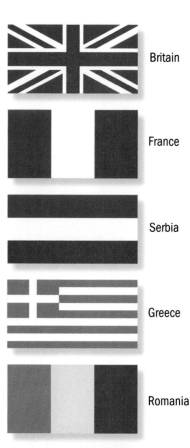

Britain

France

Serbia

Greece

Romania

 Portugal

Belgium

 Australia

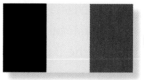 Canada

 Germany

Submarine ▶

◀ Gas mask

▲ Fighter airplane

▲ Tank

BEFORE YOU GO ON . . .

1. What were the names of the two groups of countries that were fighting against each other?

2. Why was World War I called the "first modern war"?

HOW ABOUT YOU?

- Have you ever seen any war movies? If so, what weapons were used?

Life in the Trenches

Soldiers dug trenches for protection from the enemy. The trenches were muddy after it rained, so soldiers put pieces of wood—called duckboards—on the ground to try to stay dry. The trenches were very hot in the summer and freezing cold in the winter. Rats and lice spread diseases such as trench fever. Soldiers spent about a week in the trenches. Then they went to a rest area where they could wash and change clothes before returning to the trenches.

Most of the fighting was at night, so soldiers often slept during the day. They wrote letters home or kept diaries. Many soldiers were homesick. They had a hard life in the trenches.

◀ The trenches stretched almost 650 kilometers (400 mi.).

The United States Enters the War

From the beginning of the war, President Woodrow Wilson wanted the United States to stay **neutral**. People in the United States were divided about the war. Many U.S. citizens were from European countries, so there was support for both sides. In 1915, Germany announced it would attack all neutral ships headed to Britain. In 1917, Germany announced **unrestricted** submarine warfare. That meant Germany's submarines attacked all foreign **cargo ships** to try to cut **supplies** to Britain. When Germany sank some U.S. ships, President Wilson declared war on Germany and joined the Allies.

---

neutral, not supporting any country or alliance in a conflict
unrestricted, without limits
cargo ships, ships that carry food and other things
supplies, things that people need for daily life

▲ U.S. President Woodrow Wilson

Germany Surrenders

By 1918, the Allies had stopped supplies from going to Germany, where people were **starving** because there was so little food. By October, the Allies defeated Bulgaria and Turkey. In November, Germany asked the Allies for an **armistice**. They signed an armistice on November 11, 1918. After more than four years, the war finally ended. Germany surrendered and a peace treaty was signed on June 28, 1919.

After the War

With the end of World War I, the map of Europe changed. Some countries, such as Germany, had to give up land. Other countries, such as Greece, gained land. Austria-Hungary and the Ottoman Empire were broken up into separate countries.

More than 65 million soldiers fought in the war, of whom more than half were killed or injured—8 million killed, 2 million dead of illness and diseases, 21 million wounded, and nearly 8 million taken prisoner or missing. More than 6 million **civilians** died, too. People hoped it would be the "war to end all wars," but it wasn't. World War II followed only twenty-one years later.

---

starving, very hungry
armistice, agreement to stop fighting
civilians, people who aren't in the army or navy

▲ Trenches were long narrow holes in the earth.

Country	Soldiers Killed
Germany	1,773,700
Russia	1,700,000
France	1,357,800
Austria-Hungary	1,200,000
British Empire	908,371
United States	116,516
Serbia	45,000

BEFORE YOU GO ON . . .

1 Why was life in the trenches hard?

2 Which country lost the most soldiers?

HOW ABOUT YOU?
- Why do you think so many civilians died?

143

Review and Practice

Reread the text. Copy the chart into your notebook. Then write a fact about each country. Use key words, such as *allies, enemy,* and *surrendered,* in some of your sentences. Edit your work in pairs.

Country	World War I Fact
Britain	*Britain formed an alliance with France.*
France	
United States	*The United States tried to stay neutral.*
Germany	
Bosnia	
Russia	
Austria-Hungary	

Compare this map to the map on page 136. Which countries gained land after World War I? Which countries lost land? Which countries are new?

▲ Europe after World War I

144

EXTENSION

Reread the text under the heading "Life in the Trenches" on page 142, and look at the picture of the soldiers in the trenches. Imagine that you are a soldier living in the trenches. In your notebook, write a letter home describing your life. What time of year is it? What do you see? What do you hear? What do you do in your free time?

DISCUSSION

Discuss in pairs or small groups.

1. Why did the war end in 1918?

2. Why do countries form alliances with each other?

3. Look at the map on page 144. How do you think the Allies stopped supplies from going to Germany?

4. Look at the cause-and-effect chart you made as you were reading the text. Talk about the causes and effects you wrote on your chart. Are your charts similar to those of your classmates?

5. Look at the painting, *Gassed*. What do you think is happening?

▲ *Gassed*, by American artist John Singer Sargent, painted in 1918–1919

In this section, you will read a letter and two poems. The letter, written by a young soldier, Frank Earley, describes his experiences in the war. The poems are based on real events and express the poets' feelings about war.

Letter Home

Sunday afternoon, 1st September, 1918

My dear Father,

It is a strange feeling to me but a very real one, that every letter now that I write home to you or to the little sisters may be the last that I shall write or you read. I do not want you to think that I am depressed; indeed on the contrary, I am very cheerful. But out here, in odd moments the realization comes to me of how close death is to us. A week ago I was talking with a man . . . who had been out here for nearly four years, untouched. He was looking forward with certainty to going on leave soon. And now he is dead—killed in a moment during our last advance. Well, it was God's will.

I say this to you because I hope that you will realize, as I do, the possibility of the like happening to myself. I feel very glad myself that I can look the fact in the face without fear or misgiving. Much as I hope to live through it all for your sakes and my little sisters! I am quite prepared to give my life as so many have done before me. All I can do is put myself in God's hands for him to decide, and you and the little ones pray for me to the Sacred Heart and Our Lady.

Well, I have not much time left and I must end. With my dear love.

Pray for me.

Your son,

Frank

---

on the contrary, it's the opposite
going on leave, having a rest from fighting
look the fact in the face, deal with the reality
misgiving, doubt
journalist, someone who writes for a newspaper, magazine, television, or radio
wound, an injury, especially made by a knife or bullet

About the Author

Frank Earley

Lance-Corporal Frank Earley was a young British **journalist**. His letters to his family were usually full of enthusiasm and excitement. It is only in this very last letter that he showed his more serious and thoughtful side. The next day Frank Earley suffered a serious **wound** to his chest and died hours later. He was nineteen.

War Poems

Can We Forget?

Can I ever forget? Can I ever forget?
Oh, God! Can I ever forget
My soldier boy's smile and the light in his eye,
With the army badge fresh on his sleeve—
The firm clasp of his hand and the warmth of his kiss
As he said, "Dear, be brave and don't grieve"?

Can I ever forget? Can I ever forget?
Oh, God! Can I ever forget
How the wealth of his spirit shone out of his face
When he knew we might see him no more,
While we watched his dear form where he stood on the deck
As the **steamer** pulled out from the shore?

Can I ever forget? Can I ever forget?
Oh, God! Can I ever forget
The long, weary days in the hospital **ward**,
The brow knot with pain and the face, wan and white,
The **fever-racked** frame and the hideous night—
The death at the left and the death at the right—
Oh, God! Can I ever forget?

Can I ever forget? Can I ever forget?
Oh, God! Can I ever forget
All the **fierce** storms that raged in the wild warfare's wake—
All the ways where my **lad** did his part—
Or the messages chill over the telegraph line,
Or the cold charge that went through his heart?

Cora Inez Keyes

U.S. corporal, 1918 ▶

---

steamer, ship
ward, patients' room
fever-racked, having a fever, or high temperature, resulting from sickness
fierce, wild
lad, boy

LITERARY ELEMENT

Sometimes words in a poem *rhyme*. Words that rhyme have the same sound, except for the beginning sound. For example, in "Can We Forget?" the words *sleeve* and *grieve* rhyme. What other words in the poem rhyme?

BEFORE YOU GO ON . . .

1 Why does Frank Earley say that every letter he writes may be the last?

2 What do you think happened to the soldier in the poem?

HOW ABOUT YOU?

• What do you find sad in the letter or poem? Why?

Grass

Pile the bodies high at **Austerlitz** and **Waterloo**.
Shovel them under and let me work—
                  I am the grass; I cover all.
And pile them high at **Gettysburg**
And pile them high at **Ypres** and **Verdun**.
Shovel them under and let me work.
Two years, ten years, and passengers ask the **conductor**:
                  What place is this?
                  Where are we now?

                  I am the grass.
                  Let me work.

                  Carl Sandburg

Austerlitz, Waterloo, Gettysburg, Ypres, Verdun, places where battles
    were fought in different wars
shovel them under, bury them
conductor, the person on a train or bus who sells tickets and
    announces stops

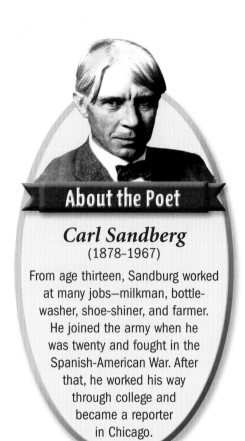

About the Poet

Carl Sandberg
(1878–1967)

From age thirteen, Sandburg worked at many jobs—milkman, bottle-washer, shoe-shiner, and farmer. He joined the army when he was twenty and fought in the Spanish-American War. After that, he worked his way through college and became a reporter in Chicago.

BEFORE YOU GO ON . . .

1. What does the grass do to the places where battles were fought?
2. What do the last two lines of "Grass" mean?

HOW ABOUT YOU?

- How does the poem "Grass" make you feel?

Link the Readings

Reread the letter and poems about World War I. Then copy the chart into your notebook and complete it. Compare your answers in small groups.

Title of Selection	Type of Text (Genre)	Purpose of Selection	How I Feel about It
"World War I"	social studies article		
"Letter Home"			
"Can We Forget?"			
"Grass"		to make people think about war and to see it in a different way	

Discuss in pairs or small groups.

1. Choose one war poem and read it aloud in pairs or small groups. Then discuss the words that express emotion. What does each part of the poem mean?

2. List five negative effects of war on people's lives. Compare your lists.

Connect to Writing

GRAMMAR

Using so as a Conjunction

Use the **conjunction so** to connect two sentences to show a result. The first sentence shows the **cause** for something, and the second sentence shows the **effect** or result. Use a comma before *so*.

cause	effect
Rats and lice lived in the trenches. Many of the soldiers got trench fever.	
Rats and lice lived in the trenches, **so** many of the soldiers got trench fever.	

cause	effect
Serbia and Russia were allies. Russia supported Serbia.	
Serbia and Russia were allies, **so** Russia supported Serbia.	

cause	effect
Tanks were heavy vehicles with big guns. They were difficult to destroy.	
Tanks were heavy vehicles with big guns, **so** they were difficult to destroy.	

Practice

Match the cause sentences to the effect sentences. Then write them in your notebook, combining them using *so*. Remember to use commas.

1. Trenches were very muddy.
2. Most fighting was at night.
3. Soldiers wrote letters home.
4. Mustard gas was a dangerous new weapon.
5. Cities and towns were bombed.
6. The Allies stopped supplies from going to Germany.

a. Many civilians died.
b. Soldiers put duckboards on the ground to keep dry.
c. Germany became weaker.
d. Soldiers often slept during the day.
e. Soldiers needed gas masks.
f. Their families knew they were still alive.

SKILLS FOR WRITING

Cause-and-Effect Organization in Writing

Sometimes a text is organized in terms of causes and effects. Here are some tips for writing a text with cause-and-effect organization:

- Think about why the event happened. This is the cause. Use the word *because* to show a cause.
- Think about what happened. This is the effect. Use the word *so* to show an effect.

Read this model. Then answer the questions that follow.

> Gabrielle Johnson
>
> Friendship
>
> Spreading rumors can cause a friendship to end. There is a girl in my school named Carrie. We used to be really close friends. However, she began to phone my friends and spread bad rumors about me. I got very upset, so I decided to confront her. When I asked her about it, she denied it. That made me even angrier with her. I stopped talking to her because I was so mad at her. Then she tried to be friends with other kids at school. She betrayed them as well, so she ended up friendless. The whole situation made me realize the effect that one small event can have on a friendship.

1. What event is discussed in the paragraph?
2. What is the cause? What is the effect?
3. What words show that the writer is using cause and effect?

WRITING ASSIGNMENT

Cause-and-Effect Paragraph
You will write a paragraph describing an event and its effects.

1. Read Reread the paragraph on page 151. Identify the causes and effects.

Writing Strategy: Cause-and-Effect Chart
Before you write your paragraph, organize your ideas. The writer who wrote the model on page 151 used this chart to organize her ideas. First, the writer wrote the causes and then she listed the effects.

Cause	→	Effect
Carrie spread bad rumors.	→	I got upset.
Carrie denied it.	→	I got angrier.
Carrie betrayed other friends.	→	She ended up friendless.

---

2. Use a cause-and-effect chart Make a chart in your notebook like the one above.

3. Write Use your chart to write your paragraph. Use the words *so* and *because* to show the relationship between causes and effects.

EDITING CHECKLIST
Did you . . .
▶ simply and clearly describe events?
▶ show the relationship between events that cause each other?
▶ use *so* and *because* to show cause and effect?
▶ use capital letters correctly?
▶ use commas and periods correctly?

Check Your Knowledge

Language Development

1. Describe cause-and-effect organization. What are two words that signal this kind of organization in a text?

2. Give an example of rhyme. In what type of text do you often find rhyme?

3. What is a cause-and-effect chart? Why is it helpful to use one?

4. Did the letter and the poems you read have anything in common? If so, what?

5. How do the map and timeline on page 136 help you understand the article "World War I"?

Academic Content

1. What new social studies vocabulary did you learn in Part 1? What do the words mean?

2. Which countries formed alliances in World War I?

3. What two changes in the map of Europe resulted from World War I?

British soldier, World War I ▶

Prepare to Read

OBJECTIVES
LANGUAGE
DEVELOPMENT

Reading:
● Vocabulary building:
  *Context, dictionary
  skills*
● Reading strategy:
  *Analyzing historical
  context*
● Text types: *Diary,
  social studies article*
● Literary element:
  Images

Writing:
● Retell a story
● Sequence-of-events
  chart
● Eyewitness report

Listening/Speaking:
● Compare and contrast
● Express opinions and
  feelings

Grammar:
● Pronoun referents

Viewing/Representing:
● Maps, illustrations,
  Venn diagram

ACADEMIC CONTENT
● Geography vocabulary
● Historical context of
  the Bosnian War
● Geography of the
  Balkans

BACKGROUND

Zlata Filipović, an eleven-year-old Bosnian girl, wrote *Zlata's Diary* in 1992, during the Bosnian War. She lived in Sarajevo, the capital of Bosnia, where some of the worst fighting occurred. She used her diary to write about her experience of day-by-day events.

Make connections The map shows the former Yugoslavia in 1991, just before the Bosnian War. Yugoslavia was a united country for many years. It had always been home to many different groups of people. During the 1980s and 1990s, long-standing conflicts caused war among different groups in Yugoslavia. As a result of the war, Yugoslavia broke up into several smaller countries: Bosnia and Herzegovina, Croatia, Macedonia, Slovenia, and Serbia and Montenegro.

Look at the map and answer the questions.

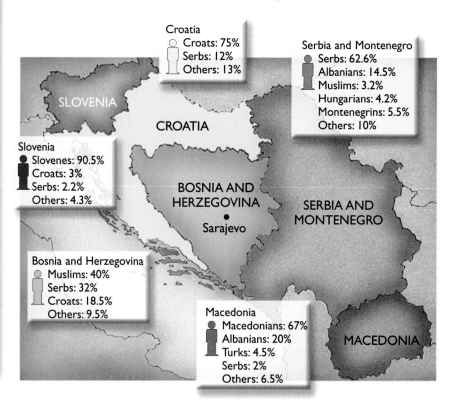

Croatia
  Croats: 75%
  Serbs: 12%
  Others: 13%

Serbia and Montenegro
  Serbs: 62.6%
  Albanians: 14.5%
  Muslims: 3.2%
  Hungarians: 4.2%
  Montenegrins: 5.5%
  Others: 10%

SLOVENIA

CROATIA

Slovenia
  Slovenes: 90.5%
  Croats: 3%
  Serbs: 2.2%
  Others: 4.3%

BOSNIA AND
HERZEGOVINA
  ● Sarajevo

SERBIA AND
MONTENEGRO

Bosnia and Herzegovina
  Muslims: 40%
  Serbs: 32%
  Croats: 18.5%
  Others: 9.5%

Macedonia
  Macedonians: 67%
  Albanians: 20%
  Turks: 4.5%
  Serbs: 2%
  Others: 6.5%

MACEDONIA

1. How many different groups of people can you see?
2. What might have caused the conflicts in Yugoslavia?

LEARN KEY WORDS

ambulance
madness
massacre
negotiate
peace
suffering

VOCABULARY

Read these sentences. Use the context to figure out the meanings of the **red** words. Use a dictionary to check your answers. Write each word and its meaning in your notebook.

1. An **ambulance** drove the sick and injured people to the hospital.
2. The war killed many people and achieved little. It was **madness**.
3. Hundreds of people were killed in the **massacre**.
4. The two presidents must **negotiate** to end the war between their countries.
5. People were happy when the war was over and there was **peace** again.
6. War causes a lot of pain and **suffering** for many people.

READING STRATEGY

Analyzing Historical Context

When we read a personal narrative, such as a diary, knowing what is happening in the background—its **historical context**—can make the text more understandable and meaningful. Historical contexts may include the political or cultural changes happening at a particular time. If the historical context is a war, this will explain some of the mood of the personal narrative and the emotions that the writer is expressing.

As you read, think about these questions:

- What is happening at the time and place where the writer is?
- What is the writer's reaction to what is happening?

As you read, think about the events that Zlata describes. How does knowing something about the historical context—in this case, war—help you to understand what Zlata is experiencing? Does it help you understand the mood?

from ZLATA'S DIARY

When Zlata Filipović wrote her diary, she was eleven years old and living in Sarajevo. The people of Sarajevo, including Zlata's family and friends, were caught in the middle of a war. Zlata calls her diary "Mimmy."

Saturday, May 23, 1992

Dear Mimmy,

I'm not writing to you about me anymore. I'm writing to you about war, death, injuries, **shells**, sadness and **sorrow**. Almost all my friends have left. Even if they were here, who knows whether we'd be able to see one another. The phones aren't working, we couldn't even talk to one another. Vanja and Andrej have gone to join Srdjan in Dubrovnik. The war has stopped there. They're lucky. I was so unhappy because of that war in Dubrovnik. I never dreamed it would move to Sarajevo. . . .

I now spend all my time with Bojana and Maja. They're my best friends now. Bojana is a year-and-a-half older than me, she's finished seventh grade and we have a lot in common. Maja is in her last year of school. She's much older than I am, but she's wonderful. I'm lucky to have them, otherwise I'd be all alone among the **grown-ups**.

▲ "I will try to get through this with your support, Mimmy. . . ."

---

shells, bombs
sorrow, sadness
grown-ups, adults

156

On the news they reported the death of Silva Rizvanbegović, a doctor at the **Emergency Clinic**, who's Mommy's friend. She was in an ambulance. They were driving a wounded man to get him help. Lots of people Mommy and Daddy know have been killed. Oh, God, what is happening here???

Love, Zlata

Tuesday, May 26, 1992

Dear Mimmy,

I keep thinking about Mirna; May 13 was her birthday. I would love to see her so much. I keep asking Mommy and Daddy to take me to her. She left Mojmilo with her mother and father to go to her grandparents' place. Their apartment was shelled and they had to leave it.

There's no shooting, the past few days have been quiet. I asked Daddy to take me to Mirna's because I made her a little birthday present. I miss her. I wish I could see her.

I was such a **nag** that Daddy decided to take me to her. We went there, but the downstairs door was locked. We couldn't call out to them and I came home feeling **disappointed**. The present is waiting for her, so am I. I suppose we'll see each other.

Love, Zlata

▲ In the beginning, the arrival of the blue berets (United Nations peacekeepers) brought hope.

Emergency Clinic, place to go for emergency medical attention
nag, someone who asks for something again and again
disappointed, sad because you expected something different

BEFORE YOU GO ON . . .

1 What happens to Silva in the ambulance?

2 Why is Zlata disappointed when she visits Mirna?

HOW ABOUT YOU?

• What do you think will happen next?

Wednesday, May 27, 1992

Dear Mimmy,

SLAUGHTER! MASSACRE! HORROR! CRIME!
BLOOD! SCREAMS! TEARS! DESPAIR!

That's what Vaso Miskin Street looks like today. Two
shells exploded in the street and one in the market.
Mommy was nearby at the time. She ran to Grandma and
Granddad's. Daddy and I **were beside ourselves** because
she hadn't come home. I saw some of it on TV but still
can't believe what I actually saw. It's unbelievable.
I've got a lump in my throat and a **knot in my tummy**.
HORRIBLE! They're taking the wounded to the hospital.
It's a **madhouse**. We kept going to the window hoping to
see Mommy, but she wasn't back. They released a list of
the dead and wounded. Daddy and I were
tearing our hair out. We didn't know what had happened
to her. Was she alive? At 4:00 Daddy decided to go and
check the hospital. He got dressed, and I got ready to go
to the Bobars', so as not to stay home alone.
I looked out the window one more time
and . . . I SAW MOMMY RUNNING
ACROSS THE BRIDGE. As she came into
the house she started shaking and crying.
Through her tears she told us how she had
seen **dismembered bodies**. All the neighbors
came because they had been afraid for her.
Thank God, Mommy is with us. Thank God.

A HORRIBLE DAY. UNFORGETTABLE.
HORRIBLE! HORRIBLE!

Your Zlata

LITERARY ELEMENT

Images are words or phrases that
create pictures in the reader's
mind. Writers use images to
describe how things look, feel,
sound, smell, and taste. What
images does Zlata use to
describe the conflict in Sarajevo?

▲ An injured woman is
taken to the hospital.

Thursday, October 1, 1992

Dear Mimmy,

Spring has been and gone, summer has been and gone, and now it's autumn. October has started. And the war is still on. The days are getting shorter and colder. Soon we'll move the stove upstairs to the apartment. But how will we keep warm? God, is anyone thinking of us here in Sarajevo? Are we going to start winter without electricity, water or gas, and with a war going on?

The "kids" are negotiating. Will they finally negotiate something? Are they thinking about us when they negotiate, or are they just trying to **outwit** each other, and leave us to our fate?

Daddy has been checking the attic and cellar for wood. It looks to me as though part of the furniture is going to **wind up** in the stove if this keeps up until winter. It seems that nobody is thinking of us, that this madness is going to go on and on. We have no choice, we have to rely on ourselves, to take care of ourselves and find a way to fight off the oncoming winter.

Mommy came home from work in a state of shock today. Two of her **colleagues** came from Grbavica. It really is true that people are being **expelled** from there. There's no sign of Mommy's and Nedo's relatives or of Lalo. Nedo is going **berserk**.

Your Zlata

▲ Cooking is quite an achievement without electricity.

---

the "kids," Zlata's slang for the politicians
outwit, be more clever than someone; trick
wind up, end up; finally be
colleagues, people you work with
expelled, forced to leave
berserk, crazy

BEFORE YOU GO ON . . .

1. How do Zlata and her father feel after the massacre on Vaso Miskin Street? Why?
2. What is the "madness" that Zlata refers to?

HOW ABOUT YOU?

• What would you do if you were in Zlata's family?

Monday, December 28, 1992

Dear Mimmy,

I've been **walking my feet off** these past few days.

I'm at home today. I had my first piano lesson. My teacher and I kissed and hugged, we hadn't seen each other since March. Then we moved on to **Czerny, Bach, Mozart, and Chopin**, to the etude, the invention, the sonata and the "piece." It's not going to be easy. But I'm not going to school now and **I'll give it my all**. It makes me happy. Mimmy, I'm now in my fifth year of music.

You know, Mimmy, we've had no water or electricity **for ages**. When I go out and when there's no shooting it's as if the war were over, but this business with the electricity and water, this darkness, this winter, **the shortage of** wood and food, brings me **back to earth** and then I realize that the war is still on. Why? Why on earth don't those "kids" come to some agreement? They really are playing games. And it's us they're playing with.

As I sit writing to you, my dear Mimmy, I look over at Mommy and Daddy. They are reading. They lift their eyes from the page and think about something. What are they thinking about? About the book they are reading

▲ Zlata gets water for her family.

---

walking my feet off, walking a lot
Czerny, Bach, Mozart, and Chopin, composers who wrote piano music
I'll give it my all, I'll do my best
for ages, for a long time
the shortage of, not enough
back to earth, not dreaming; in reality

or are they trying to put together the **scattered** pieces of this war puzzle? I think it must be the **latter**. Somehow they look even sadder to me in the light of the oil lamp (we have no more wax candles, so we make our own oil lamps). I look at Daddy. He really has lost a lot of weight. The scales say twenty-five kilos, but looking at him I think it must be more. I think even his glasses are too big for him. Mommy has lost weight too. She's shrunk somehow, the war has given her **wrinkles**. God, what is this war doing to my parents? They don't look like my old Mommy and Daddy anymore. Will this ever stop? Will our suffering stop so that my parents can be what they used to be—cheerful, smiling, nice-looking?

This stupid war is destroying my childhood, it's destroying my parents' lives. WHY? STOP THE WAR! PEACE! I NEED PEACE!

I'm going to play a game of cards with them!

Love from your Zlata

---

scattered, in many different places
latter, the second of two things mentioned
wrinkles, lines in the face

▲ Sarajevo

About the Author

Zlata Filipović

In December 1993, Zlata Filipović escaped to Paris, where she began to study at the International School. Her diary has been translated into more than twenty languages.

With the money from her book, Zlata helped to start a charity for victims of the Bosnian War. Zlata was awarded the Special Child of Courage Award.

BEFORE YOU GO ON . . .

1. What has Zlata started studying again?
2. Why is Zlata worried about her parents?

HOW ABOUT YOU?

- If you met Zlata, what questions would you ask her?

Review and Practice

Reread the excerpts from *Zlata's Diary*. Write the five dates she writes about in your notebook. Then write something important that happened on each of these days. Compare what you write in pairs or small groups.

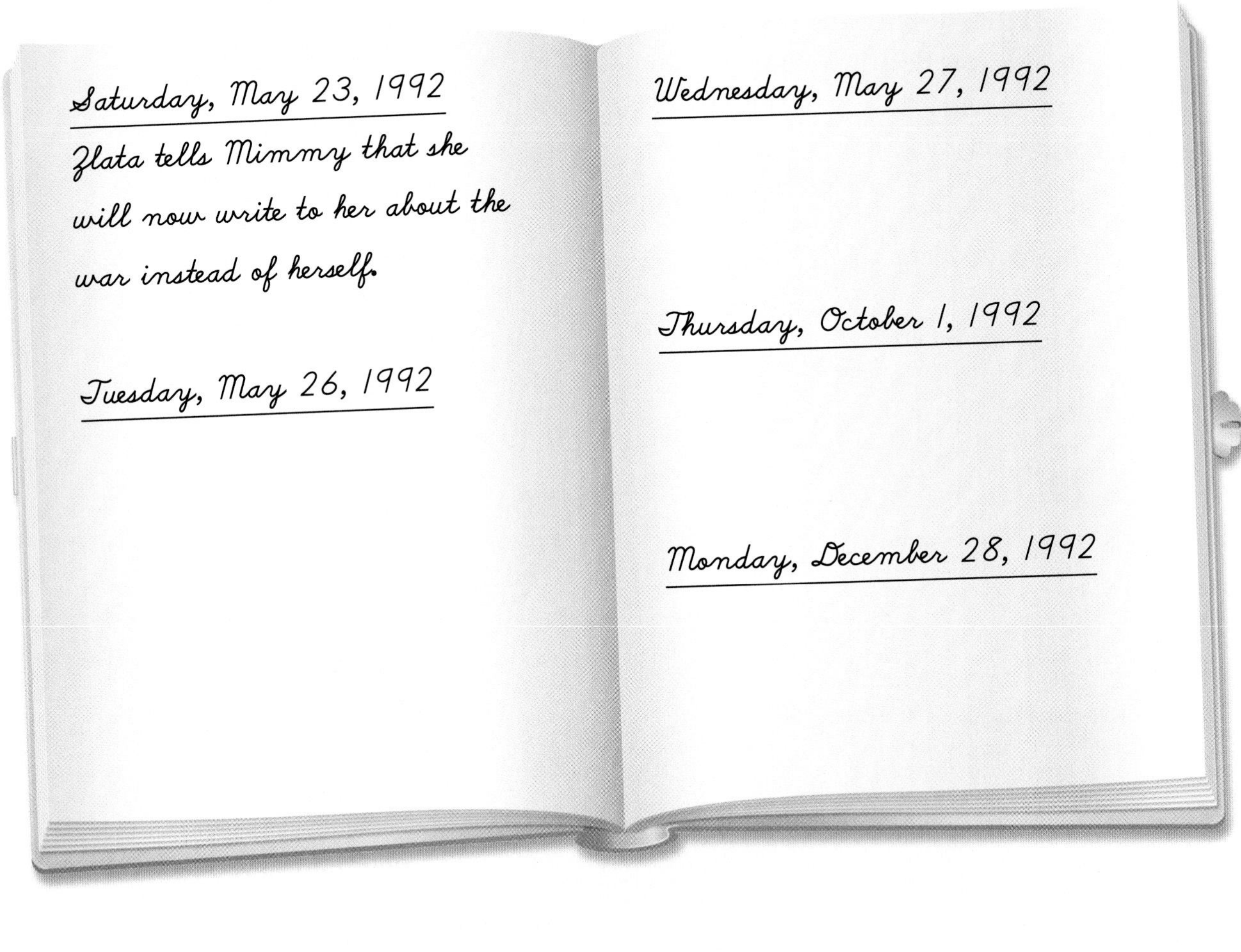

Saturday, May 23, 1992
Zlata tells Mimmy that she
will now write to her about the
war instead of herself.

Tuesday, May 26, 1992

Wednesday, May 27, 1992

Thursday, October 1, 1992

Monday, December 28, 1992

How is Zlata similar to you? How is she different? Copy the diagram into your notebook and complete it. Then compare your diagrams in pairs.

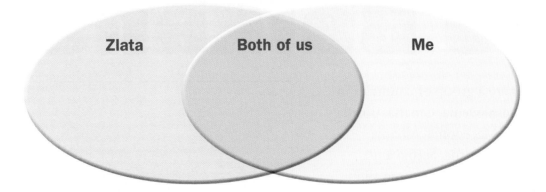

Zlata   **Both of us**   **Me**

Discuss in pairs or small groups.

1. What is the worst day of the war for Zlata? Why?
2. What kind of emotions does Zlata express in her diary?
3. Describe Zlata. What kind of person is she? Do you admire her?
4. Talk about what was happening around Zlata. How would you have felt if you were she?
5. What are some images that you remember after reading Zlata's diary entries?

◀ Zlata writes at her desk, as the sound of guns echoes from the hills.

Social Studies

This is an informational text about the geography of the Balkans. Is it fiction or nonfiction? As you read about the different places, try to find them on the map.

The Physical World: The Balkans

The Balkans are a group of countries in southeast Europe. Slovenia, Croatia, Bosnia and Herzegovina, Macedonia, Albania, Greece, Bulgaria, Romania, Serbia and Montenegro, and part of Turkey are all in the Balkans.

The word *Balkans* comes from an old Turkish word that means "mountains." The Balkans is a good name for the area because it has so many mountains.

The Balkans form a land bridge between Europe and Asia. Since ancient times, this area has been the border between the empires of the East and the West. People from different **ethnic** groups traveled through the region and settled in the hills and valleys of the region. The mountains made it difficult for the different groups of people to **interact** with each other. Therefore, many different languages, cultures, and customs developed. These differences have led to many conflicts in the area. The Balkans are often called "the **powder keg**" of Europe" because many wars have started there.

▲ The western Balkans are in southeast Europe.

BEFORE YOU GO ON . . .

1. Why are there many different languages, cultures, and customs in the Balkan region?
2. Look at the map on page 165. What is the longest river? What is the highest mountain?

HOW ABOUT YOU?

- How are the Balkans similar to where you live? How are they different?

---

ethnic, cultural
interact, communicate; do things together
powder keg, something that is ready to blow up at any time

THINGS TO LOOK FOR ON THIS MAP

Longest river: Sava, Slovenia/Croatia/Bosnia and Herzegovina/Serbia; 938 km (583 mi.)

Highest point: Triglav, Slovenia; 2,864 km (9,395 ft.)

Largest lake: L. Scutari, Montenegro/Albania, maximum size 531 sq. km (205 sq. mi.)

AUSTRIA

HUNGARY

ROMANIA

Mura R.

Drava R.

Triglav
Kranj
Nova
Gorica
SLOVENIA
Koper
Rijeka
Maribor
Velenje
Ptuj
Celje
Varazdin
Ljubljana
Koprivnica
Bjelovar
Zagreb
Virovitica
Karlovac
Sisak
Ogulin
Kupa R.
Drava R.

CROATIA
Nova
Gradiska
Dakovo
Osijek
Vukovar
Slavonski Brod

Subotica
Kanjiza
Sombor
Apatin
Backa Topola
Vojvodina
Zrenjanin
Novi Sad
Vrsac

Pula

Gospić

Zadar

Sibenik

Split

Prijedor
Bosanska
Gradiska
Bihać
Banja Luka
Kljuc
BOSNIA and
HERZEGOVINA
Jajce
Zenica
Livno
Visoko
Konjic
Foca
Mostar
Metković
Trebinje
Dubrovnik
Modrica
Doboj
Gracanica
Tuzla
Zvornik
Srebrenica
Bosna R.
Sarajevo
Neretva R.

Sabac
Loznica
Valjevo
Belgrade
Smederevo
Pancevo
Pozarevac
Velika Plana
Kolubara R.
Arandelovac
Cacak
Kragujevac
Kraljevo
Krusevac
SERBIA and
MONTENEGRO
Novi Pazar
Priboj
L. Zlatar
Bijelo Polje
Ivangrad
Niksić
Podgorica
L. Scutari
Bar
Peć
Kosovska
Mitrovica
KOSOVO
Prizren
Pristina
Gnjilane
Urosevac
NORTH ALBANIAN
ALPS
Shkod r
Drim R.

Danube R.

Zajecar

BULGARIA

Aleksinac
Nis
Leskovac
BALKAN MTS.

Kumanovo
Skopje
Tetovo
Gostivar
Kicevo
Kocani
Veles
Stip
MACEDONIA
Kavadarci
Prilep
Strumica
Vardar R.
Crna R.
Ohrid
Bitola
L. Ohrid
L. Prespa
Durr s
Shkumbin R.
Tirana
Elbasan
ALBANIA
Fier
Berat
Korc
Vlor
Vijose R.
Devoll R.

DINARIC ALPS
DALMATIA
ADRIATIC SEA

ITALY

GREECE

▲ The western Balkans

The two main religions in the Balkans are Christianity and Islam. The people of the Balkans speak many different languages: Albanian, Greek, Serbian, Croatian, Hungarian, Macedonian, Turkish, Slovenian, Bulgarian, and Romanian.

The Balkan region is a land of many contrasts. It has ancient and modern cities, beautiful mountains and rivers, as well as the scars of war, as these photos show.

▼ Danube River, Serbia

Dubrovnik, Croatia ▶

Sarajevo, the capital of Bosnia and Herzegovina ▶

BEFORE YOU GO ON . . .

1 What geographic features do you see in the photos?

2 What are some signs of war in the photos?

HOW ABOUT YOU?

● Which photo interests you the most? Why?

166

Link the Readings

Reread the text on the Balkans and think about the excerpts from *Zlata's Diary*.
Copy the chart into your notebook and complete it.

Title of Selection	Type of Text (Genre)	Fiction or Nonfiction	Purpose of Selection	What I Learned
From *Zlata's Diary*		*nonfiction*		
"The Physical World: The Balkans"			*to inform*	

DISCUSSION

Discuss in pairs or small groups.

1. How does Zlata feel about war? How do you feel about it?

2. What do you find most interesting about the Balkans?

3. Does learning about the geography of the Balkans help you understand the region's history? Explain.

4. Which reading did you enjoy more? Why?

A worker repairs a
building in Sarajevo. ▶

167

Connect to Writing

GRAMMAR

Using Pronoun Referents

Pronouns replace and refer to nouns. There are two types of pronouns: **subject pronouns** and **object pronouns**.

	Subject Pronouns	Object Pronouns
Singular	I, you, he, she, it	me, you, him, her, it
Plural	we, you, they	us, you, them

Subject pronouns replace nouns that are subjects. In this sentence, *It* refers to *Balkans*.

> subject ← → subject
> ***Balkans*** is a Turkish word. **It** means "mountains."

Object pronouns replace nouns that come after the verb. In this sentence, *it* refers to *a diary*.

> object ← → object
> Zlata wrote a **diary**. Many people have read **it**.

A **singular pronoun** (*he, she, it*) refers to a singular noun. A **plural pronoun** (*them*) refers to a plural noun.

Practice

Copy these sentences into your notebook. Draw an arrow from each underlined pronoun to the noun that it refers to. Then check your answers in pairs.

1. The mountains are beautiful. <u>They</u> are steep and rocky.
2. Zlata wrote her diary in Croatian. People have translated <u>it</u> into many languages.
3. Do you know my brother? <u>He</u> goes to your school.
4. Please write to Marta and Silva. Tell <u>them</u> to come.
5. Alana Jost is a doctor. <u>She</u> works in the hospital.
6. The bomb did not explode. Soldiers removed <u>it</u>.

SKILLS FOR WRITING

Writing Eyewitness Reports

An eyewitness report is a type of expository writing. It explains something from the point of view—or "eyes"—of someone who witnessed, or saw, something happen. A good eyewitness report:

- answers the five *wh-* questions: *Who* was involved? *What* happened? *When* did it happen? *Where* did it happen? and *Why* did it happen?
- uses sequence words to show the order in which things happened
- uses interesting details to help readers visualize
- uses pronouns to replace some nouns

Read this eyewitness report. Then answer the questions that follow.

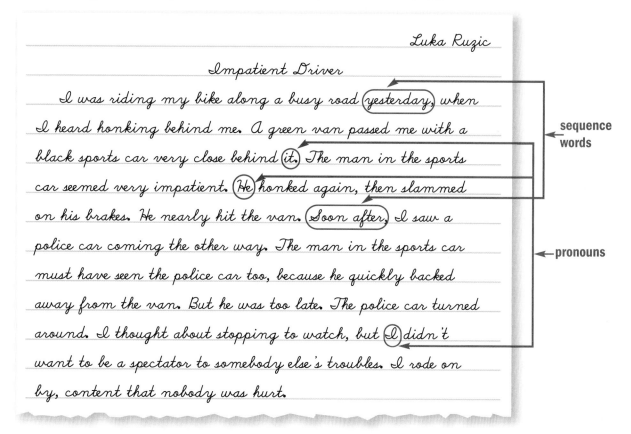

Luka Ruzic

Impatient Driver

I was riding my bike along a busy road (yesterday,) when I heard honking behind me. A green van passed me with a black sports car very close behind (it.) The man in the sports car seemed very impatient. (He) honked again, then slammed on his brakes. He nearly hit the van. (Soon after,) I saw a police car coming the other way. The man in the sports car must have seen the police car too, because he quickly backed away from the van. But he was too late. The police car turned around. I thought about stopping to watch, but (I) didn't want to be a spectator to somebody else's troubles. I rode on by, content that nobody was hurt.

sequence words

pronouns

1. What event does the writer describe? Who was involved in this event?
2. When did the event happen? Where did it happen? Why did it happen?
3. Find a sentence with a subject pronoun. What noun does it refer to?

WRITING ASSIGNMENT

Eyewitness Report

You will write an eyewitness report about a real or imaginary event.

1. **Read** Reread the eyewitness report on page 169. Note how all the sentences describe the past.

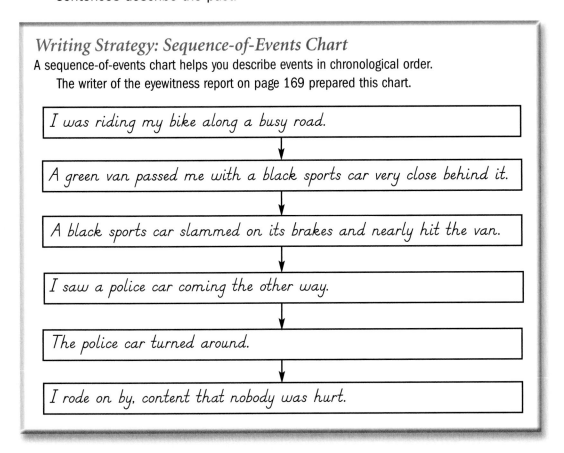

Writing Strategy: Sequence-of-Events Chart

A sequence-of-events chart helps you describe events in chronological order.
   The writer of the eyewitness report on page 169 prepared this chart.

| I was riding my bike along a busy road. |
| A green van passed me with a black sports car very close behind it. |
| A black sports car slammed on its brakes and nearly hit the van. |
| I saw a police car coming the other way. |
| The police car turned around. |
| I rode on by, content that nobody was hurt. |

2. **Make a sequence-of-events chart** Choose a real or imaginary event. Make a chart for your eyewitness report in your notebook. Complete the chart, showing the events in chronological order.

3. **Write** Use your chart to write an eyewitness report in the simple past.

EDITING CHECKLIST
Did you . . .

▶ answer the five *wh-* questions: *Who? What? When? Where?* and *Why?*

▶ describe events in chronological order?

▶ use interesting details?

▶ use pronouns correctly?

Check Your Knowledge

Language Development

1. Why is it important to analyze the historical context when reading some texts?

2. What five *wh-* questions do you answer in an eyewitness report?

3. How can a sequence-of-events chart help you write an eyewitness report?

4. Make up two sentences, one with a subject pronoun and one with an object pronoun.

5. How do maps help you understand the article "The Physical World: The Balkans"?

Academic Content

1. What new social studies vocabulary did you learn in Part 2? What do the words mean?

2. What are two effects of war that Zlata describes in her diary?

3. Name three countries in the Balkans. What are some of the geographical features of the Balkans?

▲ Montenegro

Put It All Together

OBJECTIVES

Integrate Skills
- Listening/ Speaking: *TV news show*
- Writing: *Report of a historical event*

Investigate Themes
- Projects
- Further reading

LISTENING and SPEAKING WORKSHOP

TV NEWS SHOW

You will present a TV news show. Report on events at your school, in your town, or in the world.

1 **Think about it** What kind of information do TV news shows include? Make a list of interesting recent events at your school, in your town, or in the world. What news would you like to tell others about?

Work in small groups. Compare your lists. Choose two or three events to use in a TV news show.

2 **Organize** Choose one person to be the news anchor (the main person who reads the news on TV). The other group members can be TV reporters. The news anchor introduces a reporter and tells what the report is about. Next, the reporter gives the eyewitness report. Then the anchor introduces the next reporter.

3 **Practice** Watch some TV news shows to help you plan what to say and how to say it. Practice your news show with your group. Try to do the whole show without stopping. Use pictures or maps to illustrate what you are reporting.

4 **Present and evaluate** Present your news show to the class. If possible, videotape your show. After each group finishes, evaluate the presentation. Discuss what made the news show interesting and enjoyable. Do you have suggestions for improvement?

SPEAKING TIPS

- Speak slowly and clearly.
- Use notes, pictures, and maps to help you remember and explain the event clearly.
- Use words that help the audience visualize the event.

LISTENING TIPS

- Listen for answers to the five *wh-* questions: *Who? What? When? Where? Why?* The answers to these questions give the speaker's main ideas in each report.
- Listen for supporting details and reasons. Ask yourself, "Did the speaker explain why these ideas are important?"

WRITING WORKSHOP

REPORT OF A HISTORICAL EVENT

A history report is a type of expository writing. It explains an important historical event. Like a news report, it answers the five *wh-* questions.

A good report includes the following characteristics:

- an interesting introduction that tells what the report is about
- information that answers *Who? What? When? Where? Why?*
- chronological organization
- a conclusion that summarizes the most important information

You will interview someone who has lived through a historical event, such as World War II, the Vietnam War, the Gulf War, a hurricane, a tornado, or an earthquake. Write a report based on the interview. Use the following steps and the model report to help you.

 Prewrite Make a list of questions to ask in your interview. Use your questions to help you choose your topic. Be sure your topic isn't too big. For example, if you are writing about a war, ask questions about a single event or time period.

Organize your list of questions into groups. Did you include the five *wh-* questions? Interview the person. During the interview, take notes on the answers.

WRITING TIPS

- When you write facts, make sure that your information is accurate. If you are not sure, check additional sources.
- Don't copy information from a book; use your own words. Be sure to cite your sources.
- When you describe a past event, focus on the most important details and interesting facts.

◀ A tornado

Before you write a first draft of your report, read the model. The student interviewed her mother, who assisted the president of the Peace Committee during the signing of the Ecuador-Peru Border Peace Treaty in 1998.

Cami Troya

From Conflict to Peace

On October 26, 1998, the presidents of Ecuador and Peru met in Brasilia, Brazil, to sign a peace treaty. The treaty ended a fifty-year-old conflict between Ecuador and Peru. The cause of the dispute was an unclear border between Ecuador and Peru. As a result of the unclear border, citizens of both countries did not know who owned land at the border.

The treaty stated that Ecuador was to be given one square mile of Peruvian territory named Tiwintza. This small piece of hilly land in the Amazon jungle was important to the people of Ecuador. During the last border war in 1995, Ecuadorian troops had defeated the stronger Peruvian army on this land.

In spite of their disagreements, Ecuador and Peru rediscovered a common historical artifact. This artifact was the spondylus shell. A long time ago, it was used as a form of currency by both Ecuador and Peru. The shell became a symbol of peace, and also a symbol of the new, positive relationship between the two countries.

The writer begins with an interesting introduction.

The conclusion summarizes important information.

2 Draft Use the model and your interview notes to write your report. If needed, use the library or Internet for more information. You can also include maps, timelines, and pictures to help readers understand your report. Combine the information from your interview with facts or details to put it in historical context.

3 Edit Work in pairs. Trade papers and read each other's reports. Use the questions in the editing checklist to evaluate each other's work.

4 Revise Revise your report. Add information and correct mistakes, if necessary.

5 Publish Share your report with your teacher and classmates.

Spondylus shell ▶

PROJECTS

Work in pairs or small groups. Choose one of these projects.

1 Draw or find pictures about World War I. Write a caption explaining what the picture shows. Then share your pictures with the class.

2 Visit a museum with a World War I display or watch a movie about World War I. Then share what you learned with your class.

3 Reread Lance-Corporal Frank Earley's letter or Zlata's diary entries. Write a script for an interview with one of them. Ask and answer *wh-* questions. Then perform the dialogue for the class.

4 Find tapes or CDs of folk music from the Balkan countries at the library. Share the music with your class.

5 Make a poster that shows the flags of countries in the Balkans. Look for them in encyclopedias or on the Internet. At the bottom of the poster, design a flag for *all* the Balkan countries. Then display your flag in the classroom.

6 Find an Internet site about the Balkans. With your teacher's help, connect your class with a class in a Balkan city like Sarajevo. Become pen pals and share information about your two countries.

A poster made by the U.S. government in 1917 ▶

Further Reading

To find out more about the theme of this unit, choose from these reading suggestions.

***Amistad,* Joyce Annette Barnes** In 1839, a young man called Cinque leads a group of Africans to take control of the slave ship *Amistad.* They want to return to their homes in Africa but instead they land in America and are sent to prison for murder. The Americans think of the Africans as property, not people. Now they must begin fighting for their freedom.

***Snow Falling on Cedars,* David Guterson** It is 1954 and Kabuo Miyamoto is on trial for murder. He is a Japanese American living on the island of San Piedro, off the northwest coast of the United States. World War II has left an atmosphere of anger and suspicion in this small community. Will Kabuo receive a fair trial? And will the true cause of the victim's death be discovered? Ishmael Chambers is the journalist covering the trial, and as the courtroom drama unfolds, he is forced to examine the conflict in his own soul.

***The Diary of a Young Girl,* Anne Frank** Anne Frank was thirteen years old when she and her family had to escape from the terrifying danger of the Nazi occupation in Holland. For two years they hid in tiny secret rooms at the back of an Amsterdam warehouse. Here Anne wrote her diary, an extraordinary and deeply moving account of her life in hiding.

***Lupita Mañana,* Patricia Beatty** Crossing over the border from Mexico to the United States is a dangerous business, but Lupita must do it. Her father has died in a fishing boat accident and her family is left in poverty. Lupita and her big brother, Salvador, smuggle themselves into the United States to earn money to support their mother and young siblings. But America is not the land of opportunity they'd hoped. A new language, hard labor, and the constant threat of migration officials make every day a challenge.

***Buried Onions,* Gary Soto** This book is an unforgettable portrait of life in a grim inner-city neighborhood as seen through the eyes of a young man desperately seeking a way out. At nineteen, all Eddie wants is to get by, hold down a job, and have a future. But trapped in a city full of poverty, crime, gang conflict, and unfulfilled dreams, Eddie finds that just staying alive is a challenge.

UNIT 5

We Can Be Heroes

PART 1

 "Heroes: Yesterday and Today"

 "Wind Beneath My Wings," Bette Midler

 Ethiopia, Sebastião Salgado

 From *Leaves of Grass*, Walt Whitman

PART 2

 From *The Diary of Anne Frank: The Play*, Frances Goodrich and Albert Hackett, with Wendy Kesselman

 Guernica, Pablo Picasso (painting), and Kids' Guernica art project

A hero is someone who does something brave. There are many kinds of heroes: firefighters rescuing people from burning buildings, a photographer risking his or her life to document dangerous events, or someone giving a kidney to a sick friend. Heroic acts can touch the lives of one person or many people.

In Part 1, you will read about real-life heroes, past and present. You will also listen to a song, read a poem, and look at photographs, all by or about heroes.

In Part 2, you will read an excerpt from a play about people who survived during part of a war because of their heroic acts and those of others. You will also learn about the heroic attempts of people to keep their freedom and independence in wartime.

Prepare to Read

OBJECTIVES

LANGUAGE DEVELOPMENT

Reading:
- Vocabulary building: *Context, dictionary skills*
- Reading strategy: *Making inferences*
- Text types: *Biography, song, poem*

Writing:
- Using a timeline
- Biography
- Self-evaluation
- Editing checklist

Listening/Speaking:
- Appreciation: *Song, poem*
- Sharing experiences

Grammar:
- Passive voice
- Time phrases

Viewing/Representing:
- Photographs, paintings
- Interpreting photographs

ACADEMIC CONTENT
- Social studies vocabulary
- Heroes in history

BACKGROUND

"Heroes: Yesterday and Today" is a social studies article. It gives biographical information about several heroic women and men who are well known in history. The text also describes some people whose work requires heroic effort and courage. These people risk their lives every day.

Make connections Look at the pictures and answer the questions.

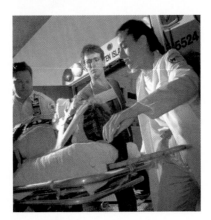
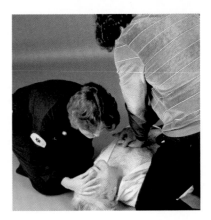

1. What is happening in each picture?
2. Why is each person heroic?
3. What are some other ways that people can be heroic?

LEARN KEY WORDS

beliefs
deeds
imprisoned
passive resistance
social justice
tolerance

VOCABULARY

Read these sentences. Use the context to figure out the meaning of the **red** words. Use a dictionary to check your answers. Write each word and its meaning in your notebook.

1. Nelson Mandela lived by his **beliefs**. Because of his refusal to abandon these ideas and values, he went to jail.
2. Mandela is internationally famous because of his brave **deeds**. He took these actions to help his people.
3. Some heroes, such as Mandela, Gandhi, and Joan of Arc, have been **imprisoned** and have spent years in jail.
4. Gandhi taught people how to show their objection to something through **passive resistance**, or nonviolent confrontation.
5. Benito Juárez was interested in **social justice**, especially the rights of native peoples.
6. People all get along better if they have greater **tolerance** for others. We have to accept other people's right to be different from us.

READING STRATEGY

Making Inferences

Fill in details, or "complete the picture" of what you are reading, by **making inferences**—combining the information in the text with your own knowledge and experience. When you make inferences, you make logical guesses and assumptions.

For example, read this sentence:

When the firefighter saw the burning house, she ran in without hesitating.

You can make the inference, or infer, that the firefighter is brave and ready to risk her life, although this is not stated in the sentence.

Making inferences whenever you read will help you understand more.

As you read, think about what you already know about these people. Then think about the new information you learn. What inferences can you make about each person or group based on what the writer tells you?

Heroes: Yesterday and Today

Joan of Arc

Joan of Arc (1412–1431) was a famous French **patriot**. Joan was a very religious child. When she was thirteen, she believed she heard God's voice telling her to help her country and fight the English, who occupied northern France.

Seventeen-year-old Joan led the French army against the English. Later, the English captured and imprisoned her. She was **burned at the stake** in 1431 when she was only nineteen. Joan of Arc was named a saint in 1920 for her heroic deeds.

Florence Nightingale

Florence Nightingale (1820–1910) came from a wealthy English family. Against her parents' wishes, she became a nurse.

In 1853, she became **superintendent** of a hospital for women in London. In 1854, Britain, France, and Turkey fought against Russia in the Crimean War. Nightingale volunteered to go to Turkey to help. She took thirty-eight nurses with her. They helped many wounded soldiers recover. Nightingale often visited the soldiers at night, carrying a lamp. Soldiers called her "The Lady with the Lamp."

When Nightingale returned to England, she started a school for nurses. The school still exists today.

▲ Joan of Arc never learned to read or write, but she was considered to be a great army leader.

▲ Florence Nightingale worked for many long hours to help the sick and dying men.

---

patriot, a person who is very loyal to his or her country
burned at the stake, put to death by tying to a post and burning
superintendent, manager; chief

Benito Juárez

Benito Juárez (1806–1872) is a national hero in Mexico. He was the son of poor Zapotec Indian farmers in the state of Oaxaca, Mexico. At age thirteen he couldn't read, write, or speak Spanish. He trained to become a priest, but later he decided to become a lawyer. As a young man, he became interested in social justice, especially the rights of native peoples. He was very popular among the native Indian population, and in 1847 he was elected governor of Oaxaca.

In 1861, Juárez became the first Zapotec Indian president of Mexico. He improved education. For the first time, it was possible for every child to go to school. He stopped the French from colonizing Mexico. His many reforms made Mexico a fairer, more modern society.

▲ Benito Juárez fought for the rights of native peoples.

Oskar Schindler

Oskar Schindler (1908–1974) was a rich German **industrialist**. During World War II, he managed a factory in Krakow, Poland. The factory made weapons for the German army. Krakow's 50,000 Jews had to live in a ghetto—a poor and crowded part of the city. Schindler saw the **brutality** of the Nazi soldiers. He said, "No thinking person could fail to see what would happen. I was now resolved to do everything in my power to **defeat** the system."

Schindler hired Jewish workers in his factory. He protected them when the Nazis tried to send them to **concentration camps**. By the end of the war he had saved about 1,300 Jews.

▲ Oskar Schindler's courageous deeds saved lives.

---

industrialist, owner or manager of a factory or industrial company
brutality, cruelty; viciousness
defeat, conquer; overcome
concentration camps, places where the Nazis killed Jews and other people in World War II

BEFORE YOU GO ON . . .

1 Why was Joan of Arc imprisoned?
2 What did Benito Juárez make it possible for all children to do?

HOW ABOUT YOU?
● Which person do you think is the most heroic? Why?

Mohandas Gandhi

Mohandas Gandhi (1869–1948) was born in Porbandar, India. At that time, India was a British colony. Gandhi went to England in 1888 and studied law. He returned to India and worked as a lawyer in Bombay (Mumbai).

In 1893, Gandhi traveled to South Africa. At that time, the government of South Africa had a system of **apartheid**. A group of white South Africans attacked Gandhi and beat him. After this experience, he encouraged people to practice passive resistance against the South African authorities and apartheid. Gandhi went to prison many times for his beliefs.

After he returned to India in 1915, Gandhi became a leader in India's struggle for independence. He became the international symbol of nonviolent protest. He believed in religious tolerance. In 1947, he negotiated an end to 190 years of British rule in India. Then, in 1948, Gandhi was assassinated by someone who didn't agree with his beliefs.

Gandhi **inspired** nonviolent movements everywhere. In the United States, his ideas about passive resistance influenced Martin Luther King Jr., when he became a leader of the Civil Rights movement in the 1950s and 1960s.

▲ Gandhi was imprisoned many times because of his beliefs.

Mother Teresa

Mother Teresa (1910–1997) was born in a part of Albania that is now in Macedonia. At age eighteen, she became a nun. She went to India in 1929. For the next twenty years, she worked as a teacher at the convent school in Calcutta. In September 1946, she "heard a voice from God." The voice told her to help poor people. She moved into one of the poorest parts of the city to teach and nurse the poor. She also set up a home for **lepers**. Mother Teresa traveled the world to talk about the terrible problems of poverty. In 1979, she won the Nobel Peace Prize.

▲ Mother Teresa with two sight-impaired children

---

apartheid, a system in which different races in a country are separated
inspired, caused; created
lepers, people with leprosy, a skin disease

184

Nelson Mandela

Nelson Mandela (1918–) is considered a great hero of the twentieth century. His country, South Africa, was ruled by a white government made up of **descendants** of English and Dutch colonists. South Africans lived under a system of apartheid. Blacks had few rights and opportunities compared to whites.

▲ Nelson Mandela speaks to people around the world.

Mandela refused to accept the suffering and injustice. He became a lawyer and joined the African National Congress (ANC) to fight for his people's rights. The government **banned** the ANC. Mandela continued to travel and speak against the government. In 1962, the government arrested him and sent him to prison, where he spent the next twenty-eight years.

Mandela said, "During my lifetime I have dedicated myself to the struggle of the African people. I have fought against white domination, and I have fought against black domination. I have cherished the ideal of a democratic and free society in which all persons live together in harmony and with equal opportunities."

In February 1990, he was finally freed from prison. The people of South Africa **abolished** apartheid in 1994, and they elected Mandela as president of South Africa.

Mandela retired in 1999 at age eighty. He is still considered a heroic figure. However, Mandela doesn't agree. He once said, "I was . . . an ordinary man who had become a leader because of extraordinary **circumstances**."

---

descendants, grandchildren, great-grandchildren, etc.
banned, made illegal
abolished, got rid of; eliminated
circumstances, events; situations

BEFORE YOU GO ON . . .

1 What were some of Mohandas Gandhi's beliefs?

2 Why is Nelson Mandela a hero?

HOW ABOUT YOU?

• What questions would you like to ask Mohandas Gandhi, Mother Teresa, and Nelson Mandela?

Doctors Without Borders

Doctors Without **Borders** is an international organization whose members believe that every person in every country has the right to medical care. It helps victims of war, diseases (such as AIDS), and natural and man-made **disasters**. A small group of French doctors started Doctors Without Borders (*Médecins Sans Frontières*) in 1971. Each year, more than 2,500 volunteer doctors, nurses, and **administrators** from eighteen countries provide medical aid in more than eighty countries. They provide health care, perform surgery, organize **nutrition** and **sanitation** programs, train local medical staff, and provide mental health care.

Doctors Without Borders works with the United Nations, governments, and the media to tell the world about their patients' suffering and concerns. For example, Doctors Without Borders volunteers told the media about the **atrocities** they saw in Chechnya, Angola, and Kosovo.

Doctors Without Borders won the Nobel Peace Prize in 1999. Accepting the award, one of the **founders**, Bernard Kouchner, said, "I'm deeply moved, and I'm thinking of all the people who died without aid, of all those who died waiting for someone to knock on their door."

▲ Nearly one-third of Angola's children—an average of 420 children every day—die before their fifth birthday of starvation or disease, as a result of the 27-year civil war.

borders, official lines that separate two countries
disasters, horrible events that cause great damage and death
administrators, people who manage businesses or organizations
nutrition, nourishment; eating healthful foods
sanitation, hygiene; cleanliness
atrocities, extremely violent actions
founders, people who start organizations or companies

▲ A doctor helps a child in a refugee camp in Somalia.

▲ Firefighters search for survivors in the ruins of the World Trade Center.

New York City Firefighters

On September 11, 2001, **hijackers** flew planes into the World Trade Center in New York City and the Pentagon outside of Washington, D.C. The planes **exploded**, and the buildings caught on fire.

At the World Trade Center, hundreds of New York City firefighters and other emergency workers ran into the burning buildings to try to save people. The fires caused the buildings to collapse. Three hundred forty-three firefighters and twenty-three police officers died. Nearly 3,000 people died in the disaster, but about 25,000 people escaped. The rescue workers saved many lives.

At a memorial ceremony for one of the firefighters, former New York City Mayor Rudolph Giuliani called September 11 the New York Fire Department's "darkest day and finest hour."

---

hijackers, people who illegally take control of an airplane
exploded, burst into fire and small pieces; blew up

BEFORE YOU GO ON . . .

1. What does Doctors Without Borders try to tell the world?
2. What buildings were hit by hijacked airplanes on September 11, 2001?

HOW ABOUT YOU?
- How do you think the name Doctors Without Borders describes the group's main belief?

Review and Practice

Reread "Heroes: Yesterday and Today." Copy the chart into your notebook. Write at least one sentence about each person or group that tells why you think they are heroic. Use what you already know about being a hero, and facts you learned in the text. Try to use some of these words: *beliefs, deeds, imprisoned, passive resistance, social justice, tolerance.*

Heroes	Why Are They Heroic?
Joan of Arc	
Florence Nightingale	
Benito Juárez	
Oskar Schindler	
Mohandas Gandhi	
Mother Teresa	
Nelson Mandela	
Doctors Without Borders	
New York City firefighters on September 11, 2001	*The firefighters tried to rescue people from the World Trade Center. They knew it was dangerous. They were probably afraid, but they did their jobs anyway.*

EXTENSION

Think about someone you believe is heroic. Write three sentences telling about the person (or group).

DISCUSSION

Discuss in pairs or small groups.

1. Which heroes spent time in prison because of their beliefs? Why?
2. Some heroes die for their beliefs. Find an example in the text, and explain.
3. Gandhi believed that passive resistance is a good way to protest against something that is unjust, or wrong. Do you agree with him? Why or why not?
4. Which of the heroes from the text would you like to meet? Why?

CONNECT TO LITERATURE

Music, Art, and Poetry

As you read this section, think about how the work of singers, photographers, and poets can influence the way we see and experience the world.

Wind Beneath My Wings

It must have been cold there in my shadow,
To never have sunlight on your face.
You were content to let me shine,
   that's your way.
You always walked a step behind.

So I was the one with all the glory,
While you were the one with all the strain.
A beautiful face without a name for so long.
A beautiful smile to hide the pain.

Chorus
Did you ever know that you're my hero,
And everything I would like to be?
I can fly higher than an eagle,
For you are the wind beneath my wings.

It might have appeared to go unnoticed,
But I've got it all here in my heart.
I want you to know I know the truth,
   of course I know it.
I would be nothing without you.

Fly, fly, fly high against the sky,
So high I almost touch the sky.
Thank you, thank you,
Thank God for you, the wind beneath my wings.

About the Artist

Bette Midler

Entertainer, environmentalist, and singer, Bette Midler was born in 1945. After studying drama at the University of Hawaii, she worked as a film extra and made her stage debut in New York City in 1966. In 1974, she won a Grammy Award for her album *The Divine Miss M*, and a Tony Award for her Broadway show of the same title. Midler is the founder of the New York Restoration Project. In June 2002, she received the Parks and Preservation Award for her commitment and generosity to New York's parks and historic sites.

◀ *Ethiopia*, by
Sebastião Salgado,
1984

Sebastião Salgado

Sebastião Salgado was once a successful economist.
Then, on a trip to Africa in 1973, he decided to become a
photographer. For many years he bravely photographed
wars and other crises for news agencies. In the 1980s, he
worked with Doctors Without Borders in the Sahel region
of Africa during a major **drought** and **famine**. Concerned
about the millions of refugees, migrants and dispossessed,
Salgado has photographed in thirty-nine countries, such as
India, Pakistan, Sudan, Congo, Ethiopia, and Angola. Why?
"My photographs . . . give the person who does not have
the opportunity to go there the possibility to look. . . ."

Salgado's photographs show people's courage and
dignity as they struggle to achieve basic human rights.
Today, he is one of the world's most respected
photographers. He has published ten books and won many
awards.

▲ Sebastião Salgado was born
in Brazil and now lives in
France.

---

drought, a time when no rain falls and the land becomes very dry
famine, grave shortage of food; starvation

BEFORE YOU GO ON . . .

1 What does "You are the
wind beneath my wings"
mean?

2 In what ways is Salgado
heroic?

HOW ABOUT YOU?
● Would you rather be a
musician or a
photographer? Explain.

from *Leaves of Grass*

I am the **mashed** fireman, with breast-bone broken . . .
    tumbling walls buried me in their **debris**—
Heat and smoke, I respired . . . I heard the yelling
    shouts of my **comrades**—
I heard the distant click of their picks and shovels.
They have cleared the **beams** away . . . they **tenderly**
    lift me forth.

Walt Whitman

---

mashed, injured
debris, broken pieces
comrades, fellow workers and friends
beams, long heavy pieces of wood or metal used in building houses
tenderly, gently

◀ New York firefighters raise the American flag among the ruins of the World Trade Center.

About the Poet

Walt Whitman

Walt Whitman (1819–1892) was born in West Hills, New York. He is considered one of the greatest American poets. His poems celebrate the dignity and freedom of the ordinary person. His book *Leaves of Grass* is one of the most famous collections of poems in American literature.

BEFORE YOU GO ON . . .

1. What happened to the firefighter in the poem?
2. How do the firefighters treat their injured comrade?

HOW ABOUT YOU?

- Why do you think the firefighters are raising the flag in the photo?

Link the Readings

In Part 1, you read several texts and looked at a photograph about heroes. Review the texts and photograph. Then copy the chart into your notebook and complete it.

Title of Selection	Type of Text (Genre)	Fiction or Nonfiction	Purpose of Selection
"Heroes: Yesterday and Today"	*biographies*		
"Wind Beneath My Wings," Bette Midler			*to entertain*
Ethiopia, Sebastião Salgado			*to inform*
From *Leaves of Grass*, Walt Whitman			

DISCUSSION

Discuss in pairs or small groups.

1. What are some qualities of heroes?

2. Can you think of a time when you had to be extra strong? What did you do? Were you surprised that you had that strength?

3. Talk about a hero that you know or have heard about. Tell why this person is heroic. Then write a few sentences in your notebook that describe your hero.

Connect to Writing

GRAMMAR

The Passive Voice

Verbs in sentences are in either the **active voice** or the **passive voice**.

active voice	passive voice
Schindler **hired** Jewish workers.	Jewish workers **were hired** by Schindler.

Use a form of *be* + past participle of the verb to form the passive voice.

Thousands of people **were saved** by the firefighters.

Use the active voice to focus on the *performer* of an action.

performer   action
Police officers **rescued** people from the collapsed buildings.

Use the passive voice to focus on the *receiver* of an action.

receiver   action
Many people **were rescued** from the collapsed buildings.

Use a *by* phrase to tell who or what performed the action. Use the *by* phrase only when it is important to know who performed the action.

Martin Luther King Jr. was influenced **by Gandhi**.

When it is not important to know who performed the action, the *by* phrase is not necessary.

Many soldiers **were wounded**.

Practice

Complete the sentences in your notebook. Use the passive forms of the verbs in parentheses. Remember to use *by* when necessary.

1. Joan of Arc _____ (burn) at the stake when she was nineteen years old.

2. More than 1,300 Jewish workers _____ (save) Oskar Schindler.

3. Benito Juárez _____ (elect) governor of Oaxaca in 1847.

4. The refugees _____ (help) Doctors Without Borders.

SKILLS FOR WRITING

Using Time Phrases to Write a Biography

In a biography, a writer usually tells events in chronological order. Writers use time phrases to show chronology and to tell when things happened. Here are some examples:

yesterday	the next day	on September 11, 2001	in 1948
at age eighty	last night	during the summer	

Read the biography below. Then discuss the questions.

A. J. Seidner

Michael Jordan: Basketball Hero

Michael Jordan was born on February 17, 1963. During his youth, Jordan enjoyed playing baseball, basketball, and football. At age fifteen, however, he was cut from the high school basketball team. But in the following years, his playing greatly improved.

Jordan was chosen to play on the U.S. Men's Olympic Team in 1984. Two months after the Olympics, he played his first season with the Chicago Bulls. He led the Bulls to three World Championships. In 1995, after a one-year retirement from the NBA, he returned, and one year later, he led the Bulls to their fourth Championship title. In 2002, he joined the Washington Wizards, continuing his legendary performances.

Michael Jordan is truly an American hero. He shows that all dreams can be realized and that persistence is the key to victory.

---

1. What time phrases does the writer use to tell when the events happened?
2. Where does the writer use the active voice? What does this show?
3. Where does the writer use the passive voice? What does this show?

WRITING ASSIGNMENT

Biography

You will write a biography of someone that you consider to be a hero.

1. **Read** Reread the biography on page 195. Then think of someone you admire and you consider to be a hero. It can be someone you know or someone you've read about.

Writing Strategy: Timeline

Biographies usually tell events in chronological order. A timeline can help you organize ideas for your biography. Look at the timeline that the writer created for a biography of Michael Jordan.

1963	1984	1994	1995	2002
born	played in Olympics; played with Chicago Bulls	retired from NBA	returned to NBA	played with Washington Wizards

1. What does each point on the timeline show?
2. Did the writer include the most important events? Would you add or subtract anything?

---

2. **Make a timeline** Make a timeline of your hero's life in your notebook. Write some important events and the years they happened. Begin with your hero's birth or with an important event early in his or her life. When you finish, exchange timelines with a partner. Discuss your timelines, and choose the most important events to write about.

3. **Write** Use your timeline to write a short biography of your hero. Remember to use the active and passive voices. Use time phrases to show the order of events and tell when things happened.

EDITING CHECKLIST

Did you . . .

▶ include the most important events?

▶ use time phrases to show the order of events and when things happened?

▶ use the active and passive voices?

▶ use correct punctuation?

196

Check Your Knowledge

Language Development

1. Describe the reading strategy of making inferences.

2. What is a biography? Is it fiction or nonfiction? Explain.

3. How are a poem and a song similar? How are they different?

4. How can a timeline help you write a biography?

5. What is the passive voice? How is it different from the active voice? Give one example of a sentence using the passive voice.

6. What is a time phrase? Why do writers use time phrases?

7. Choose one of the photographs in Part 1 and describe it. Why do you think it is included in a unit about heroes and heroic acts?

Academic Content

1. What new social studies vocabulary did you learn in Part 1? What do the words mean?

2. Why is Florence Nightingale called "The Lady with the Lamp"?

3. What do Gandhi and Mandela have in common?

Florence Nightingale ▶

PART 2 Prepare to Read

OBJECTIVES

LANGUAGE DEVELOPMENT

Reading:
- Vocabulary building: *Context, dictionary skills*
- Reading strategy: *Visualizing*
- Text types: *Play, social studies article*
- Literary element: *Recognizing and analyzing setting*

Writing:
- Book or movie review
- Self-evaluation
- Editorial checklist

Listening/Speaking:
- Retelling a story
- Comparing and contrasting

Grammar:
- Comparative and superlative adjectives

Viewing/Representing:
- Interpreting paintings

ACADEMIC CONTENT
- Social studies vocabulary
- World War II
- Spanish Civil War

BACKGROUND

The play, *The Diary of Anne Frank*, is based on the book *Anne Frank: The Diary of a Young Girl*. Anne Frank wrote her diary in Amsterdam, Holland, between 1943 and 1945 while hiding from the Nazis during World War II.

People who write plays are called playwrights. Actors usually perform plays for an audience. The script of a play has dialogue and stage directions. The dialogue is the words the actors speak. The stage directions are the words in parentheses in the script. They tell how the actors should look, move, and speak.

Make connections Anne Frank and her family hid in secret rooms, called the annex, for over two years. They had to be very quiet during the day so no one would hear them. They couldn't leave the annex. They depended on Mr. Frank's work colleagues to bring them food and other necessities. These people heroically risked their lives to help the family.

Look at the pictures of the hiding place. Then answer the questions.

▲ The secret annex was at the back of Mr. Frank's office building.

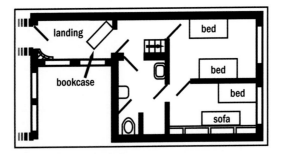

1. Imagine you had to live here for two years with six other people. How would you feel?
2. What would you miss the most about the outside world?

VOCABULARY

Read these sentences. Use the context to figure out the meaning of the **red** words. Use a dictionary to check your answers. Write each word and its meaning in your notebook.

LEARN KEY WORDS

destination
forbidden
go into hiding
identity
impression
regulations

1. The family left Germany—their **destination** was Holland.
2. Jewish children were **forbidden** to go to school with non-Jewish children. They had to go to special Jewish schools.
3. Many Jews had to **go into hiding** to escape the Nazis.
4. Her **identity** was secret. No one knew who she was.
5. Anne's diary gives the **impression** that she was older than she really was.
6. If people didn't obey the Nazis' **regulations**, they were punished.

READING STRATEGY

Visualizing

Visualizing means getting mental images, or pictures in your mind, from a text. You learned about this reading strategy in Unit 2, when you read an excerpt from the novel *A Boat to Nowhere*.

When reading a play, use the stage directions to help you visualize the action, the characters, and the surroundings, or setting. Stage directions are usually in parentheses. For example:

(She looks down the steps where Peter van Daan, a shy, awkward boy of sixteen, wearing a heavy coat with the conspicuous yellow star, waits nervously. He is carrying a cat in a basket.)

One of the rooms in the annex ▼

199

As you read this excerpt from the play, try to visualize the action, characters, and setting. Use the stage directions to help you.

from The Diary of Anne Frank

The Play

Frances Goodrich and Albert Hackett, with Wendy Kesselman

On June 12th, 1942, Anne Frank received a diary for her thirteenth birthday. A few weeks later, on July 6th, the family was forced to move into the secret annex. They lived there for two years with the van Pels family (Anne calls them the van Daans in her diary) and another Jewish man. Mr. Frank's former work colleagues, Mr. Kraler and Miep Gies, helped the families survive.

ANNE: *(Voiceover)* July sixth, 1942. A few days ago, Father began to talk about going into hiding. He said it would be very hard for us to live **cut off** from the rest of the world. He sounded so serious I felt scared. "Don't worry, Anneke. We'll take care of everything. Just enjoy your **carefree** life while you can." *(She pauses.)*

Carefree? I was born in Frankfurt on June twelfth, 1929. Because we're Jewish, my father **emigrated**

---

cut off, separated
carefree, without worries
emigrated, left one's own country to live in another

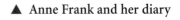
▲ Anne Frank and her diary

to Holland in 1933. He started a business, manufacturing products used to make jam. But Hitler **invaded** Holland on May tenth, 1940, a month before my eleventh birthday. Five days later the Dutch surrendered, the Germans arrived—and the trouble started for the Jews. *(A pause.)*

Father was forced to give up his business. We couldn't use streetcars, couldn't go to the theater or movies anymore, couldn't be out on the *street* after 9 P.M., couldn't even sit in our own gardens! We had to turn in our bicycles; no beaches, no swimming pools, no libraries—we couldn't even walk on the sunny side of the streets! My sister Margot and I had to go to a Jewish school. Our identity cards were stamped with a big black "J". And . . . we had to wear the yellow star. But somehow life went on. Until yesterday, when a call-up notice came from the **SS**. Margot was ordered to report for work in Germany, to the **Westerbork transit camp**. A call-up: Everyone knows what that means! *(She pauses.)*

At five-thirty this morning, we closed the door of our apartment behind us—ten days earlier than my parents had planned. My cat was the only living creature I said goodbye to. The unmade beds, the breakfast things on the table all created the impression we'd left in a hurry. *(A pause.)*

And our destination? We walked two and a half miles in the pouring rain all the way to . . . Father's office building! Our hiding place, the "Secret Annex," is right behind it upstairs. Even though the Germans forced Father out, he still runs the office with Mr. Kraler and Miep, who've agreed to help us while we're in hiding. *(As Mr. Frank pulls a large **tarpaulin** off the kitchen table, he sees a rat move across the floor. Mrs. Frank shrieks.)*

---

invaded, entered a place using military force
SS, high-ranking members of the Nazi Party
Westerbork transit camp, a place in Holland where people were put on trains to the concentration camps
tarpaulin, a piece of material used to cover and protect an object

LITERARY ELEMENT

The *setting* is the time and place of the action in a story or play. To recognize, or identify, the setting, ask yourself when and where the story takes place.

When analyzing, or thinking about, the setting, consider all the details the writer gives about the time and place.

BEFORE YOU GO ON . . .

1 Why do the Franks go into hiding?
2 Who helps them?

HOW ABOUT YOU?

• Imagine you have to go into hiding. What would you take with you?

201

MRS. FRANK: A rat!

MR. FRANK: Shhh! (*Quickly he motions her to be quiet, as Miep comes up the steps.*)

MR. FRANK: Ah, Miep!

MIEP: Mr. Frank. Thank God you arrived safely.

ANNE: Miep!

MIEP: Anne. Margot. (*As Margot and Mrs. Frank slowly sit up.*) Mrs. Frank, you must be exhausted. If only we'd known we would have had it all ready for you.

MR. FRANK: You've done too much already, Miep. Besides, it's good for us to keep busy. As you see, Anne's my little helper.

MIEP: I can see that. (*She looks down the steps where Peter van Daan, a shy, awkward boy of sixteen, wearing a heavy coat with the* **conspicuous** *yellow star, waits nervously. He is carrying a cat in a basket.*) Peter—come in!

MR. FRANK: (*Quickly coming forward.*) Peter. The first to arrive. (*Shaking his hand.*) Welcome, Peter. Peter van Daan, children.

ANNE: (*Rushing toward him.*) Welcome to the Annex!

MR. FRANK: Peter—Margot, Anne. You already know Mrs. Frank.

PETER: (**Solemnly** *shaking hands with Mrs. Frank.*) Mrs. Frank.

MRS. FRANK: Forgive me, Peter. I'm not quite myself. But I'm so glad you'll be with us.

MARGOT: I am too.

ANNE: (*Looking down at the basket.*) A cat! (*Turning to Margot.*) He has a cat!

PETER: (*Self-conscious.*) A black one.

ANNE: We have a cat too. I wanted to bring her but . . . (*Glancing at her mother.*) I know our neighbors will take care of her till we come back. I don't know what I'll do without her. But it'll be great having a cat here. Won't it, **Pim**? Won't it be fantastic?

MRS. FRANK: Anne dear, don't get so excited. Peter doesn't know you yet.

ANNE: (*Laughing.*) He'll get to know me soon though. It's going to be so much fun having people around. A whole other family. Won't it, Margot?

MARGOT: Yes.

ANNE: (*Skipping around the room.*) Like being on vacation in some strange **pension** or something. An adventure— **romantic** and dangerous at the same time!

MR. FRANK: (*Watching Peter's* **anxious** *face.*) What is it, Peter?

PETER: My parents. They were right behind me, one street away.

MR. FRANK: (*Laying his hand on Peter's shoulder.*) They'll be here.

PETER: You don't think they were . . .

MRS. FRANK: Don't worry, Peter. (*Smiling.*) You're just like me.

---

conspicuous, very easy to notice
solemnly, seriously or sadly

self-conscious, shy; awkward
Pim, Anne's nickname for her father
pension, a hotel or boarding house
romantic, emotional and dreamlike
anxious, worried

▲ Margot (left) and Anne

▲ Peter

The Frank family ▶

▲ The entrance
to the annex,
hidden by a
bookcase

Anne at school ▶

BEFORE YOU GO ON . . .

1 How does Anne feel about hiding in the annex?

2 Why is Peter anxious about his parents?

HOW ABOUT YOU?

• Is Anne like you in any way? If so, how?

203

ANNE: Mother's always jumping at every little thing. (*Peeking into Peter's basket.*) What's its name?

PETER: (*Self-conscious.*) Mouschi.

ANNE: (*To the cat.*) Mouschi! Mouschi. I love cats. (*To Peter.*) Where'd you go to school?

PETER: They set up a **technical school** in someone's house, once we were forbidden—

ANNE: (*Breaking in.*) I had to switch from my Montessori school to the Jewish Lyceum.

PETER: I know. I saw you there.

ANNE: You did? (*Mr. Kraler hurries up the stairs with Mr. and Mrs. van Daan. Mrs. van Daan is wearing a fur coat and carrying an umbrella and a large hat box. Mr. van Daan carries a **satchel** and his briefcase. All three are out of breath.*)

MR. FRANK: (*To Peter, smiling.*) See— what did I tell you? Now we're all here.

MR. KRALER: (*Obviously shaken.*) Just in time. We had to take the long way around—there were too many **Green Police** on the streets. (*Mr. van Daan breaks open a package of cigarettes, nervously starts smoking.*)

MR. FRANK: (*Shaking hands with the van Daans.*) Welcome, Mrs. van Daan. Mr. van Daan. You know my wife, of course, and the children. (*Mrs. Frank, Margot and Anne shake hands with the van Daans.*)

MR. KRALER: We must hurry. The workmen will be here in half an hour.

MR. FRANK: Such trouble we're causing you, Mr. Kraler, after all you and Miep have done. And now we arrive early!

MR. KRALER: You couldn't let your daughter be taken away, Mr. Frank.

MIEP: Please don't worry. We will do everything we can to help you. Now I must run and get your **ration books**.

MRS. VAN DAAN: Wait—if they see our names on ration books, they'll know we're here, won't they?

MIEP: Trust me—your names won't be on them. I'll be up later. If you make a list every day, I'll try to get what you want. And every Saturday I can bring five library books. (*She hurries out.*)

MR. FRANK: Thank you, Miep.

ANNE: Five! I know what my five are going to be.

MRS. FRANK: Anne, remember, there are seven of us.

ANNE: I know, Mother.

MARGOT: (*Troubled.*) It's **illegal**, then, the ration books? We've never done anything illegal.

MR. VAN DAAN: I don't think we'll be living exactly according to regulations here. (*The **carillon** is heard playing the quarter hour before eight.*)

ANNE: Listen. The Westertoren!

---

technical school, a school that teaches auto mechanics, machine repair, and other skills
satchel, a small bag for carrying clothing, books, etc.
Green Police, Dutch police who supported the Nazis

ration books, booklets of coupons that allow people to buy food during wartime
illegal, not allowed by law
carillon, bells on a clock tower

MRS. FRANK: How will I ever get used to that clock?

ANNE: Oh, I love it!

MR. KRALER: Miep or I will be here every day to see you. I've hidden a **buzzer** to signal you when we come up, and tomorrow I'll have that bookcase placed in front of your door. Oh, and one last thing . . . the radio . . . *(He points to a small radio hidden beneath a sheet.)*

ANNE: *(Bounding over to the radio.)* A radio! Fantastic!

MRS. VAN DAAN: A radio. Thank God.

MR. VAN DAAN: How did you get it? We had to turn ours in months ago.

MR. FRANK: Thank you, Mr. Kraler. For everything. *(Mr. Kraler turns to go, as Anne drops a batch of silverware.)*

MR. KRALER: *(To Mr. Frank.)* Oh . . . you'll tell them about the noise?

MR. FRANK: I'll tell them.

MRS. FRANK: *(Following Mr. Kraler to the top of the stairs.)* How *can* we thank you really? How can we ever—

MR. KRALER: I never thought I'd live to see the day a man like Mr. Frank would have to go into hiding. *(He hurries out, as she stands still, watching him.)*

*** * ***

On August 4, 1944, the secret annex was raided by the Security Police. Anne and the seven others in hiding were arrested. They were transported to Auschwitz concentration camp. After a month there, Anne and Margot were sent to Bergen-Belsen concentration camp, where they both got typhus, a deadly disease. They died within a short time of each other in March 1945, only a few weeks before the camp was liberated by the British. Only Anne's father Otto Frank survived. In 1947, he published Anne's diary.

About the Authors

Frances Goodrich and Albert Hackett

Frances Goodrich and Albert Hackett wrote the screenplays for some of Hollywood's most famous movies. *The Diary of Anne Frank*, written in 1955, was perhaps their greatest achievement. Wendy Kesselman's version, based on an expanded and unedited version of the original diary, portrays a more realistic Anne.

---

buzzer, a small device that makes a loud noise

BEFORE YOU GO ON . . .

1 How will Miep and Mr. Kraler signal that they are coming up to the annex?

2 Why do you think Anne is so excited about the radio?

HOW ABOUT YOU?

• Do you like Anne? Why or why not?

Review and Practice

Reread the excerpt from *The Diary of Anne Frank.* Number the events in chronological order. Remember that some of these events took place before the two families moved into the annex.

_____ The Frank family welcomes Peter.

_____ Jews in Holland are forced to wear a yellow star.

_____ Anne sees the cat Mouschi for the first time.

_____ The Frank family walks two and a half miles in the pouring rain.

____1____ Hitler invades Holland, and the Dutch surrender.

_____ Miep offers to bring library books to the families.

Now use your list to retell the story to a partner.

◄ Anne's diary

1. The excerpt from *The Diary of Anne Frank* describes the first day of life in hiding for the two families. What did you visualize as you read? Draw a picture of what you visualized and share it with the class.

2. Visualize yourself in the Secret Annex, hiding with the two families. How do you feel after a year? Copy the chart into your notebook. Make a list of things that are difficult for you. For example, think about things you can't do because you are hiding. Make another list of things you have learned. Share your ideas with a partner. How are your lists similar and different?

What Is Difficult	What I've Learned

DISCUSSION

Discuss in pairs or small groups.

1. When the Germans invaded Holland, how did life change for Anne and her family?

2. What are some things that Miep and Mr. Kraler have to worry about?

3. What do you think life was like in the annex after a year? Do you think Anne was still happy? Why or why not?

Art, Social Studies

This is an informational text. It tells about the Spanish Civil War, and about some ways that war inspires artists. Is it fiction or nonfiction?

Does Pablo Picasso's Guernica *tell you how he feels about war? Can you tell from the painting* Hiroshima *how the students feel about war and peace?*

Heroic Art

Guernica

During the Spanish Civil War (1936–1939), Spain was a divided country. A large group of Spaniards hated General Franco, Spain's fascist **dictator**. This group was called the Resistance. The Resistance wanted to defeat Franco's government, but Franco was a powerful leader. Franco was supported by Hitler (the leader of Nazi Germany) and Mussolini (the leader of fascist Italy). The Resistance made Franco very angry.

At this time, Guernica, a town in northern Spain, had a population of 7,000. Guernica was independent and democratic. On April 26, 1937, Franco ordered Nazi planes to bomb the town. It was 4:00 P.M. on a busy market day. About 1,650 innocent people were killed and 889 were injured.

---

dictator, a ruler who has complete power over a country

> **Picasso's symbols**
> the bull = the brutality of war
> the horse = the people
> the electric light = an all-seeing God
> the flower = hope

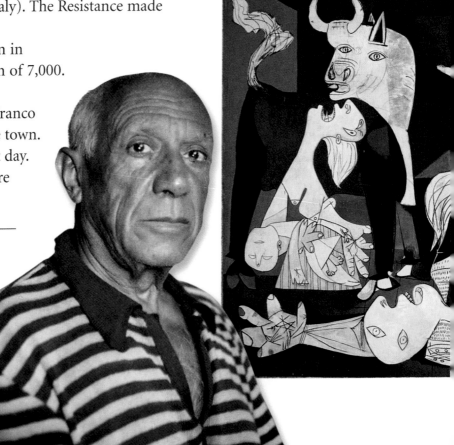

Pablo Picasso ▶

208

Pablo Picasso

Picasso (1881–1973) was one of the most important artists of the twentieth century. He was born in Spain and moved to Paris when he was twenty-three.

After the bombing of Guernica, Picasso was shocked by the black-and-white photographs he saw in the newspapers. He quickly sketched the first images for a mural. *Guernica* shows the horror and **chaos** of war.

Picasso wrote this **prose-poem** about the bombing of Guernica.

> *. . . cries of children cries of women cries of birds cries of flowers cries of timbers and of stones cries of bricks cries of furniture of beds of chains of curtains of pots and of papers cries of odors which claw at one another cries of smoke pricking the shoulder of cries . . .*

BEFORE YOU GO ON . . .

1. What happened to the town of Guernica?
2. How did Picasso feel about war?

HOW ABOUT YOU?

- How does the painting *Guernica* make you feel?

---

chaos, confusion
prose-poem, descriptive writing that is similar to poetry

▲ Pablo Picasso painted *Guernica* in 1937. It is a powerful statement about war.

▲ *Hiroshima*, by students participating in the Kids' Guernica art project

Kids' Guernica

Kids' Guernica is an international art project for peace. In 1995, Yasuda Tadashi started the project in Kyoto, Japan. Using the Internet, Tadashi organized schools around the world to participate in the project. His idea was for children in different parts of the world to create peace paintings on huge **canvases** the same size as Pablo Picasso's *Guernica*. Children participate in workshops in their schools and create their paintings. So far, more than 500 children from schools in Cambodia, Sri Lanka, Chile, Nepal, India, Algeria, Germany, the United States, Australia, China, Canada, France, Italy, and other countries have participated. Their paintings express powerful messages of peace.

In 1945, the United States dropped an **atomic bomb** on the city of Hiroshima, Japan, ending World War II. The city was completely destroyed. In 1999, forty-one students from four elementary schools in Hiroshima participated in the Kids' Guernica art project. These schools are all located in the area where the bomb exploded. The students created their mural in memory of the 140,000 people who died and to express their hope for peace in the future.

---

canvases, strong cloths on which artists paint pictures
atomic bomb, a weapon that causes a huge explosion and kills many people

BEFORE YOU GO ON . . .

1 What is the Kids' Guernica art project?

2 What message do you think the painting *Hiroshima* expresses about war and peace?

HOW ABOUT YOU?

● Would you like to participate in Kids' Guernica? If so, what would you paint?

Link the Readings

Reread "Heroic Art" and think about the excerpt from *The Diary of Anne Frank*. Copy the chart into your notebook and complete it.

Title of Selection	Type of Text (Genre)	Fiction or Nonfiction	Purpose of Selection	Heroic Act
From *The Diary of Anne Frank*				
"Heroic Art"	*informational text*			*defending one's beliefs; giving one's life for a cause*

DISCUSSION

Discuss in pairs or small groups.

1. Study the paintings on pages 208–210. What words or expressions describe these two pictures? Make two lists comparing the paintings. Share your lists with the class.

2. Imagine that Anne Frank made a painting after two years in the annex. What are some things you think she would put in her painting?

3. Review the list of Picasso's symbols on page 208. Do you see any symbols in *Hiroshima*, on page 210? Can you think of other symbols that artists use in their work?

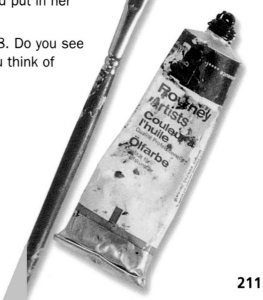

Connect to Writing

GRAMMAR

Comparative and Superlative Adjectives

Use **comparative adjectives** to compare two things.

> Margot is **older than** Anne.
> Paris is **more famous than** Guernica.

Use **superlative adjectives** to compare three or more things.

> Peter is **the oldest** of all three children.
> Paris is **the most famous** city in France.

Make the comparative/superlative forms of one-syllable adjectives like this:

Adjective	Comparative	Superlative
old	old**er than**	**the** old**est**
young	young**er than**	**the** young**est**

Make the comparative/superlative forms of adjectives of two or more syllables like this:

Adjective	Comparative	Superlative
famous	**more** famous **than**	**the most** famous
heroic	**more** heroic **than**	**the most** heroic

Some adjectives have irregular comparative and superlative forms.

Adjective	Comparative	Superlative
good	**better than**	**the best**
bad	**worse than**	**the worst**

Practice

Complete the sentences in your notebook. Use comparative or superlative adjectives.

1. Anne Frank was _____ person in the annex. (young)

2. Anne's diary is _____ book ever written by a young girl. (famous)

3. The annex was _____ room in the house. (small)

4. Margot was _____ Anne. (tall)

212

SKILLS FOR WRITING

Writing Reviews

A review is a type of persuasive writing. A review gives the writer's opinion about a movie, a book, a play, an exhibition. A review includes:

- the writer's opinion: does he or she like or dislike the work?
- examples that support the opinion: what was good or bad?
- the writer's recommendation: does he or she suggest that you see or read the work?

Read the review. Then discuss the questions that follow.

> Adam Chodoff
>
> <u>Billy Stargate and the Space Heroes:</u> The Movie
>
> The movie <u>Billy Stargate and the Space Heroes</u> was not as good as the book, though it did have its fun parts. First of all, the movie was more fast-paced than the book because many scenes were cut out. For example, the movie didn't include many of the scenes in which Billy is investigated by the space police. In the book, these scenes helped to create the mood for the story. However, the movie's outer space scenes were more exciting than the ones in the book. The wonderful special effects made them extremely exciting. Overall, I thought the book was better than the movie. It's not the greatest movie I've seen, but it's fun.

1. What is the writer's opinion of the work?
2. What reasons does he give to support his opinion?
3. Where does the writer use comparative or superlative adjectives? What do they compare?

WRITING ASSIGNMENT

Review

You will write a one-paragraph review of a book, movie, or TV show.

1. **Read** Reread the movie review on page 213. Note how the writer used comparative and superlative adjectives.

Writing Strategy: T-Chart

Before you write your review, think about what you liked and didn't like about the movie, book, or TV show. One way to do this is to make a T-chart.

Look at the T-chart that the writer created for his review of *Billy Stargate and the Space Heroes* on page 213.

What I Liked	What I Didn't Like
Movie was more fast-paced than the book.	Movie was less interesting than the book.
Special effects made parts of movie more exciting than the book.	Some important parts were left out. Some of the story's mood was lost.

---

2. **Make a T-chart** Make a T-chart in your notebook. On one side of the T-chart, list what you liked about the movie, book, or TV show. On the other side, list what you didn't like about it. Look at the number of ideas in each list. The list with the most ideas tells you whether you liked or didn't like the movie, book, or TV show.

3. **Write** Use your T-chart to write your review. In the first sentence, give your opinion—whether you liked it or not. Then write your ideas supporting your opinion. End your review by recommending the movie, book, or TV show, or not, to your readers.

EDITING CHECKLIST

Did you . . .

▶ include the name of the book, movie, or TV show in your title?

▶ indent the first line of the paragraph?

▶ state your opinion clearly?

▶ give reasons that support your opinion?

▶ use comparative or superlative adjectives correctly?

▶ use correct punctuation?

214

Check Your Knowledge

Language Development

1. How do you use visualizing when you read a play? When you read a novel?

2. What is setting? Give an example.

3. What is an example of a comparative adjective? When do you use this form of adjective?

4. What is an example of a superlative adjective? When do you use this form of adjective?

5. What kind of things do you think about when you interpret a painting? Give an example, using one of the paintings in Part 2.

6. How can a T-chart help you write a review?

Academic Content

1. What new social studies vocabulary did you learn in Part 2? What do the words mean?

2. What do you know about the Spanish Civil War? Who was the Spanish dictator at the time?

3. What happened in the town of Guernica? Why did Pablo Picasso paint *Guernica*?

4. What is the Kids' Guernica art project? What do the children's paintings express?

Put It All Together

OBJECTIVES

Investigate Skills
- Listening/
  Speaking:
  Speech
- Writing:
  *Letter to the
  editor*

**Investigate
Themes**
- Projects
- Further
  reading

LISTENING and SPEAKING WORKSHOP

SPEECH

You will give a persuasive speech about an after-school program to improve your school.

1 **Think about it** What kinds of after-school programs would help students at your school? Make a list of possible programs. Work in small groups. Discuss your lists. Which programs would help the greatest number of students? Choose one.

2 **Organize** Work together to write a speech about your after-school program. In the speech, include the name of your program, the main purpose for it, and the reasons that it would be good for the school. Choose a group speaker to give the speech to the class.

3 **Practice** Listen carefully to your group speaker as he or she practices the speech. Give the speaker ideas to make the speech better.

4 **Present and evaluate** Give your group's speech to the class. After each speaker finishes, evaluate the speech. Were the speaker's arguments persuasive? Vote to decide which after-school program is the best. Consider presenting the idea to your principal or your parent-teacher group.

SPEAKING TIPS

- Write important ideas of your speech on note cards. Write just a few words in big letters on each card. Use the cards to help you remember your main ideas.
- Speak clearly and slowly. You might use gestures to emphasize important ideas.
- End your speech by restating the main purpose of your after-school program.

LISTENING TIP

When people want to persuade you to do something, they often give only arguments that support their position or point of view. As you listen to a speech, think about the opposite point of view. Then draw your own conclusions.

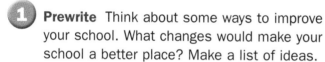

WRITING WORKSHOP

LETTER TO THE EDITOR

People write letters to a newspaper editor to express their opinions. Sometimes a letter to the editor includes an idea for solving a problem or improving something in the community. The writer uses arguments to persuade the reader of his or her opinion and idea.

A good letter to the editor includes the following:

- an opening paragraph with a clear statement of the writer's opinion

- reasons or arguments that support the writer's opinion, presented in a clear, organized way

- a concluding paragraph that restates the writer's opinion in a different way

You will write a persuasive letter to the editor of your school newspaper. Use the following steps and the model on page 218 to help you.

1 **Prewrite** Think about some ways to improve your school. What changes would make your school a better place? Make a list of ideas.

Look at your list. Next to each idea, write how it would make your school better. For example, who would be helped by the idea or change? Then review your ideas, and choose one idea to write about in a letter to the editor.

Make a T-chart. Over the left column write *For*, and over the right column write *Against*. In the *For* column, give arguments that support your idea. In the *Against* column, give arguments that don't support your idea.

WRITING TIP

Transition words connect ideas and make your arguments more persuasive. Look at how these transition words are used:

- ***In addition,*** some of the bike racks are broken.
- ***Besides*** being good exercise, bike riding is fun.
- ***Futhermore,*** bikes do not cause air pollution like buses and cars.
- ***Another*** argument in favor of more bike racks is safety.

Before you write a first draft of your letter, read the following model. Notice the characteristics of a letter to the editor.

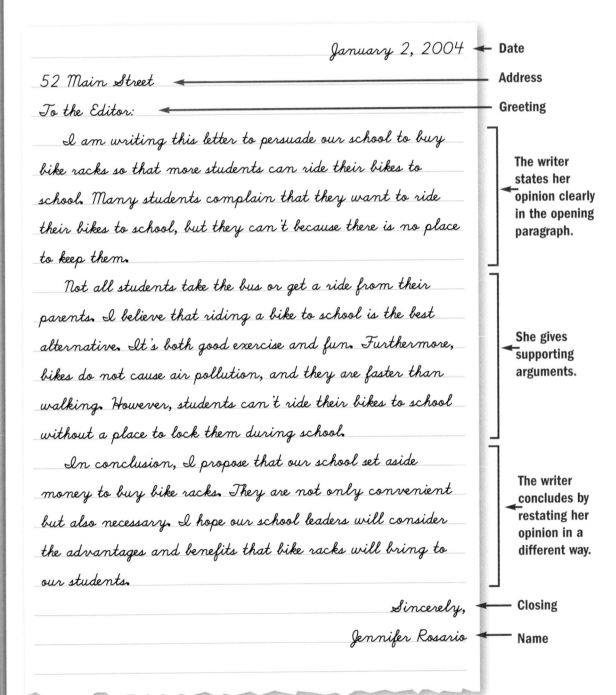

January 2, 2004 ← **Date**

52 Main Street ← **Address**

To the Editor: ← **Greeting**

I am writing this letter to persuade our school to buy bike racks so that more students can ride their bikes to school. Many students complain that they want to ride their bikes to school, but they can't because there is no place to keep them.

The writer states her opinion clearly in the opening paragraph.

Not all students take the bus or get a ride from their parents. I believe that riding a bike to school is the best alternative. It's both good exercise and fun. Furthermore, bikes do not cause air pollution, and they are faster than walking. However, students can't ride their bikes to school without a place to lock them during school.

She gives supporting arguments.

In conclusion, I propose that our school set aside money to buy bike racks. They are not only convenient but also necessary. I hope our school leaders will consider the advantages and benefits that bike racks will bring to our students.

The writer concludes by restating her opinion in a different way.

Sincerely, ← **Closing**

Jennifer Rosario ← **Name**

2 **Draft** Use your T-chart and the model to write your letter to the editor. Use your supporting arguments to persuade readers to agree with your idea.

3 **Edit** Work in pairs. Trade papers and read each other's letters. Use the questions in the editing checklist to evaluate each other's work.

EDITING CHECKLIST

Did you . . .

▶ state your opinion clearly in the first paragraph?

▶ include arguments that support your opinion?

▶ use comparative and superlative adjectives correctly?

▶ use transition words at the beginning of some sentences?

▶ restate your opinion in the last sentence?

▶ use correct form for writing a letter to the editor?

4 **Revise** Revise your letter. Add information and correct mistakes if necessary.

5 **Publish** You may want to send your letter to the school newspaper. If your school doesn't have one, create a class newspaper on a computer. Include as many letters as you can.

PROJECTS

Work in pairs or small groups. Choose one of these projects.

1. Find biographies of different heroes in the library or on the Internet. Choose a person from the past or the present and read about his or her life. Give an oral report about your hero to the class.

2. Find some books about or photographs of famous photographers in the library or on the Internet. For example, some famous American photographers are Margaret Bourke-White, Dorothea Lange, Walker Evans, and Gordon Parks. Choose a photographer and look at his or her work. Choose one or two photographs that you really like. Show the photographs to the class, and explain why you like them.

3. Do a readers theatre. Take the full script of *The Diary of Anne Frank: The Play* out of the library. Let group members choose the characters they want to be. Practice reading the play together several times. Help each other get the words just right. Then present your readers theatre to the class.

▲ Anne with Mr. Frank in the play, *The Diary of Anne Frank.*

4. Think about how Picasso expressed strong feelings in his painting *Guernica*. Choose a person, place, or thing that you feel strongly about. Paint or draw a picture that expresses your feelings about your subject. Share your picture with the class.

5. With a family member, look through newspapers or magazines for pictures of heroes. Make a scrapbook that contains the stories of a few people that you think are heroic. Share your scrapbook with your class.

6. Make a thank-you card for a hero in your community. Tell the person how you feel about his or her heroic deed. Ask your teacher to help you find the person's address so that you can mail your card.

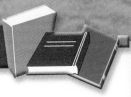

Further Reading

To find out more about the theme of this unit, choose from these reading suggestions.

Free At Last, The Story of Martin Luther King Jr., **Angela Bull** This is a biography of civil rights leader Martin Luther King Jr., who encouraged nonviolent protest to fulfill his dream of an America where people would be judged by "the content of their character, not by the color of their skin."

Joan of Arc, **Angela Bull** Learn more about the amazing story of a young peasant girl in the fifteenth century who believed that she was being directed by the voices of saints to lead the French to freedom in battle against the occupying English.

The Red Badge of Courage, **Stephen Crane** This classic tale of the American Civil War follows the fortunes of a proud young soldier, Henry Fleming, who quickly learns that there is much more to war than adventure and bravery.

The Barefoot Book of Heroic Children, **Rebecca Hazel** Is it possible for children to make a difference in the world? What children have influenced the course of history and what can we learn about them? This book brings together the stories of some of the most amazing young people in history, and gives inspiring accounts of their optimism and ideals in the face of great suffering and hardship.

We'll Never Forget You, Roberto Clemente, **Trudie Engel** Roberto Clemente was an unforgettable baseball hero. When he was growing up in Puerto Rico, his family didn't have enough money to buy baseballs or baseball bats. So he learned to play by hitting tin cans with a broomstick. Later, he became one of the greatest hitters in the history of the game.

6

LOOK INTO THE
FUTURE

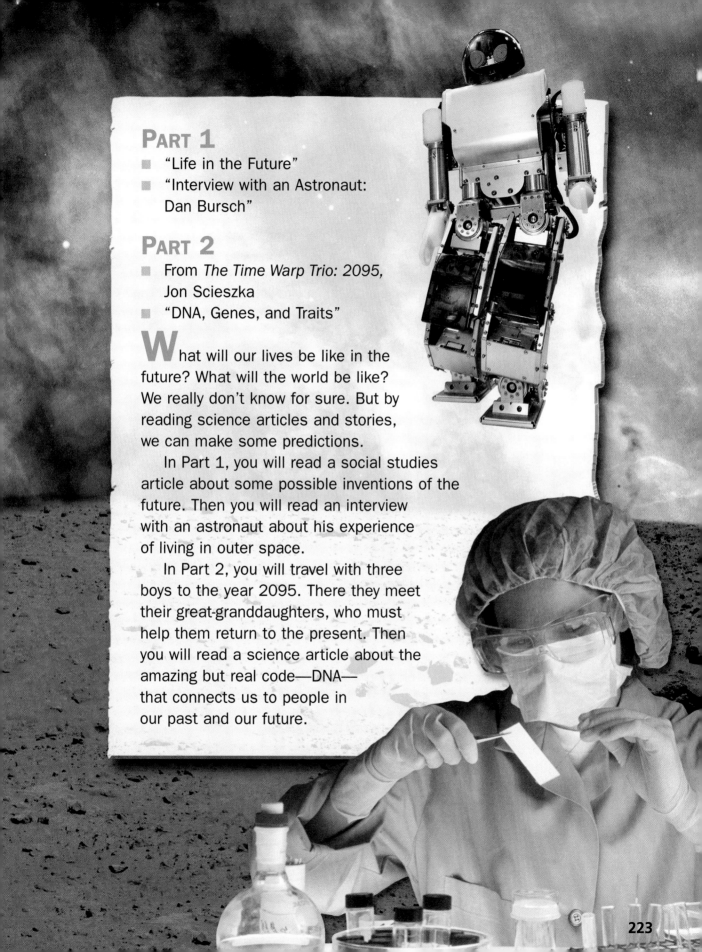

PART 1

- "Life in the Future"
- "Interview with an Astronaut: Dan Bursch"

PART 2

- From *The Time Warp Trio: 2095*, Jon Scieszka
- "DNA, Genes, and Traits"

What will our lives be like in the future? What will the world be like? We really don't know for sure. But by reading science articles and stories, we can make some predictions.

In Part 1, you will read a social studies article about some possible inventions of the future. Then you will read an interview with an astronaut about his experience of living in outer space.

In Part 2, you will travel with three boys to the year 2095. There they meet their great-granddaughters, who must help them return to the present. Then you will read a science article about the amazing but real code—DNA— that connects us to people in our past and our future.

223

Prepare to Read

OBJECTIVES

**LANGUAGE
DEVELOPMENT**

Reading:
- Vocabulary building: *Context, dictionary skills*
- Reading strategy: *Summarizing*
- Make observations about text
- Text types: *Social studies article, interview*

Writing:
- Subtopic web
- Taking notes
- Research report

Listening/Speaking:
- Compare and contrast
- Ask for and give information

Grammar:
- Future: *Will*

Viewing/Representing:
- Timeline
- Future images and inventions

ACADEMIC CONTENT
- Social studies vocabulary
- Life in the future
- Comparison of Earth and Mars

BACKGROUND

"Life in the Future" is a social studies article. It tells what some scientists think life will be like in the future. It is nonfiction—it uses facts to describe what will be happening years from now.

Make connections   Look at these pictures of a telephone, a car, some children, and an airplane from the past. Then answer the questions.

1. Compare the telephone, car, clothes, and airplane with those of today. How are they similar? How are they different?
2. How do you think telephones, cars, clothes, and airplanes will be different in the future?

LEARN KEY WORDS

artificial
frontier
mass produced
population
robots
traffic jams

VOCABULARY

Read these sentences. Use the context to figure out the meaning of the **red** words. Use a dictionary to check your answers. Write each word and its meaning in your notebook.

1. Doctors sometimes use **artificial** hearts to replace diseased hearts.
2. Outer space is sometimes called a **frontier** because we know so little about it.
3. Cars are no longer made one at a time—they are **mass produced**.
4. The **population** of Earth will increase greatly. There will be billions more people in the next 100 years.
5. Human beings won't need to do dangerous work in the future because **robots** will do the work.
6. **Traffic jams** are the result of too many cars on the road.

READING STRATEGY

Summarizing

Summarizing helps you remember important information in a text. It also helps you check to see if you understand what you are reading.

When you summarize, you retell the text's main ideas. A summary is always much shorter than the text. When you write a summary, use some words from the text and some of your own words. As you choose the information you want to summarize, keep in mind your reason for reading the text.

Before you summarize, ask yourself these questions:

- What happened?
- What are the main ideas?

225

Science, Social Studies

Preview and skim the text and set your purpose for reading. Then, as you read more carefully, write a sentence or two after each section summarizing the main ideas of that section.

Life in the Future

Imagine traveling in a time machine into the future. What do you think life will be like? This timeline shows some predictions about the future.

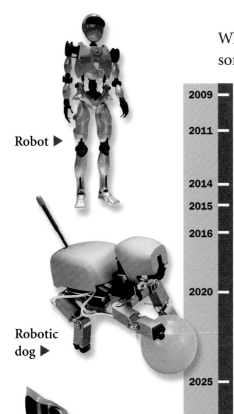

Robot ▶

Robotic dog ▶

◀ Artificial leg

2009	fire-fighting robots that can find and rescue people
2011	clothes that become cooler or warmer depending on the outside temperature
2014	robotic pets
2015	telephone calls between speakers of different languages translated in real time
2016	humans traveling to Mars
2020	cars that drive themselves on automated highways; artificial lungs, kidneys, and brain cells
2025	underground cities
2030	more robots than people in some countries
2035	fully functioning artificial eyes and legs; people **cured** of 98% of all cancers

cured, healed; restored to health

The Growing World

The world's population is growing very fast. In 1800, the population was about 1 billion. Now it is over 6 billion. One reason for this fast growth is that the birth rate is higher than the death rate. That is, there are more people being born than there are people dying. Also, medical advances and better living conditions help people live longer. Scientists predict that in the year 2100, the population will be 11 billion.

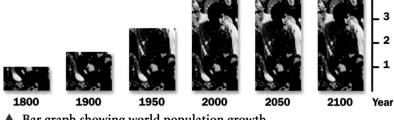

Population in billions

▲ Bar graph showing world population growth

Future Cities

As the population grows, it will be necessary to rebuild existing cities and build new ones. Some apartment buildings will be like small cities.

Architects have created a model for an apartment building in Tokyo. It will be 840 meters (2,750 ft.) high and will have 180 floors. A population of 50,000 will be able to live there. High-speed **elevators** will carry eighty people at a time. The building will have stores, restaurants, and cinemas. People won't ever have to leave!

◀ Model for an apartment building in Toyko

---

elevators, machines in a building that carry people from one floor to another

BEFORE YOU GO ON . . .

1. Look at the timeline. What new inventions do experts predict?
2. What do they predict the population will be in 2050?

HOW ABOUT YOU?

- What new inventions do you want to have in the future?

227

Cars of the Future

As more people own cars, the roads become more crowded. This causes more traffic jams and more accidents. The cost of traffic jams in the United States is about $78 billion per year— 4.5 billion hours of travel time plus 26 billion liters (7 billion gal.) of fuel wasted sitting in traffic.

Car manufacturers are always looking for ways to make cars safer, faster, and more convenient. In the future, there may be automated highways. On these highways, cars will **steer** themselves. They will go faster and brake by themselves. Cars will have computers that pick up signals from **magnets** in the road.

What about flying cars? Flying cars may fill the skies in the future. Paul Moller has spent forty years and millions of dollars developing his Skycar. He is now close to completing the first successful flying car, the Skycar M400. Computers and satellites will control it. The Skycar will cost about $1 million. Once it is mass produced, however, the price could be as low as $60,000.

▲ An artist's idea of transport in the future

---

steer, guide
magnets, pieces of iron that attract other pieces of iron

◀ Skycar M400 will be able to reach a speed of 560 kilometers (350 mi.) per hour.

▲ The X-43A will be the first plane to reach hypersonic speeds using an air-breathing engine.

Hypersonic Planes

The National Aeronautics and Space Administration (NASA) is developing a hypersonic plane. A hypersonic plane will be able to fly five times faster than the speed of sound, and it will be able fly to outer space. NASA produced a $185 million **prototype** plane in April 2001. But it doesn't expect to use the hypersonic plane for space travel until about 2020.

The X-43A prototype plane looks like a flying surfboard. It is thin and has a wingspan of 1.5 meters (5 ft.). It is 3.6 meters (12 ft.) long and weighs 1,270 kilograms (2,800 lbs). A working version of the X-43A will be about 60 meters (200 ft.) long.

prototype, the first model

BEFORE YOU GO ON . . .

1. Give an example of what a car of the future will do.
2. What is a hypersonic plane?

HOW ABOUT YOU?

- Do you think a flying car is a good idea? Why or why not?

Jetpacks

People have always dreamed of flying. In the fifteenth century, the Italian artist Leonardo da Vinci drew many designs of flying machines. But a personal flying machine—or jetpack—has proved to be one of the most difficult inventions.

Jetpacks have appeared in such movies as *The Rocketeer, Spy Kids,* and *Minority Report.* A "rocket man" flew into the opening ceremony of the 1984 summer Olympics in Los Angeles. Jetpacks today can fly for only a short time. In the future, they will fly longer and go faster.

The most successful jetpack prototype is the SoloTrek Exo-Skeletor Flying Vehicle (XFV). The XFV uses propellers to lift you off the ground. Once in the air, you can **zip** over treetops at 130 kilometers (80 mi.) per hour for 240 kilometers (150 mi.) before **refueling**.

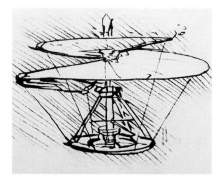

▲ Leonardo da Vinci designed flying machines in the 1400s.

---

zip, move very fast
refueling, refilling with fuel

▲ The SoloTrek Exo-Skeletor Flying Vehicle (XFV) can climb as high as 3,000 meters (10,000 ft.). ▶

New Frontiers

Throughout history, humans have loved to explore. Today, we have explored most of our planet. There are few new lands to explore. But there are new worlds, new planets, and new **galaxies**.

In the future, perhaps we will **colonize** other planets. The most likely planet will be Mars. NASA scientists have already sent probes—spacecraft without people—to explore Mars. But when will people be able to go there? Astronauts could travel to Mars by about 2015. But it will be a difficult task! It will take six months to reach Mars. (It takes only three days to reach the moon.) And Mars is not a friendly **environment**. Mars probably once had liquid water, but now it is a cold, rocky desert. It has the largest volcano in the solar system and the deepest canyons. Dust storms can cover the whole planet. There is no breathable **oxygen**.

For people to live on Mars, the cities will have to be protected from the **poisonous** air. Giant **domes** will have to be built to control the atmosphere. All food will have to be grown inside the domed cities.

▲ An artist's idea of a colony on Mars

Earth–Mars Comparison

	Earth	Mars
Average distance from sun	150 million kilometers (93 million mi.)	228 million kilometers (142 million mi.)
Length of year	365.25 days	687 Earth days
Length of day	23 hours 56 minutes	24 hours 37 minutes
Temperature	average 14°C (57°F)	average –63°C (–81°F)
Atmosphere	nitrogen, oxygen, argon, others	mostly carbon dioxide, some water vapor
Number of moons	1	2

galaxies, very large groups of stars
colonize, set up human communities
environment, the land, water, and air
oxygen, a gas in the air that all plants and animals need in order to live
poisonous, deadly
domes, round roofs

BEFORE YOU GO ON . . .

1. What is an example of a new frontier that humans can explore?
2. Look at the Earth–Mars Comparison chart. Which planet is farther away from the sun? Which planet has only one moon?

HOW ABOUT YOU?

- Would you like to travel to Mars? Why or why not?

Review and Practice

Reread "Life in the Future." Copy the chart into your notebook. Write a one-sentence summary of each section. Try to use the key words—*artificial, frontier, mass produced, population, robots,* and *traffic jams*—in your summary.

Section	Summary
The Growing World	*Scientists predict that the world population will grow to 11 billion by the year 2100.*
Future Cities	
Cars of the Future	
Hypersonic Planes	
Jetpacks	
New Frontiers	

Now use your summary to tell a partner about "Life in the Future."

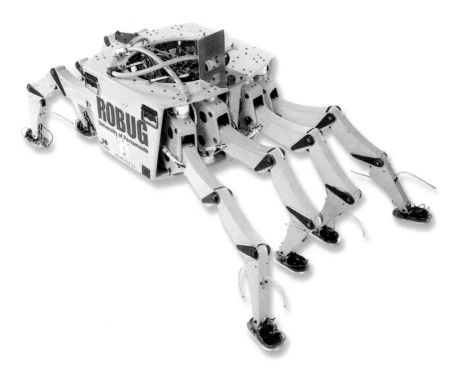

EXTENSION

1. Pretend that you are living in the future. Write a paragraph about what a typical day is like for you. Where do you live? How do you get around? What kind of clothes do you wear? You can use some of the inventions described in "Life in the Future," or you can create your own inventions. Exchange your paragraph with a partner. How are your future lives similar and different?

2. What are some jobs you think robots will have in the future? Make a list.

DISCUSSION

Discuss in pairs or small groups.

1. Why would people have to live in giant domes on Mars?

2. What would you like about living on the 180th floor of an apartment building? What wouldn't you like about it?

3. Would you rather live 100 years in the future or 100 years in the past? Why?

4. Do you think robots should do some jobs that people now do? Why or why not?

An artist's idea of a space colony of the future, where 10,000 people will live and work ▶

Interview

In this section, you will read an interview. In an interview, one person—the interviewer (or, in this case, interviewers)—asks questions, and another person answers. For this interview, students used the Internet to ask an astronaut about his work. As you read, think about the main topics that the students ask about.

Interview with an Astronaut: Dan Bursch

*Dan Bursch has made three space flights and has been in space for 746 hours. He lived on the International Space Station from December 5, 2001 until June 19, 2002. Before this expedition, he **chatted** online with some students on www.discovery.com.*

▲ Dan Bursch

Dan Bursch: I would just like to say welcome to everyone tonight. Thank you for spending your Sunday evening with me. . . .

Cody: I am ten years old, and I would like to know what the food is like. I would also like for you to trade me just one day in the space station and you can go to my school.

Dan Bursch: Well, thanks, Cody. Food is very important for us up in space, as it is here on Earth. In fact, one of the things that I will be starting tomorrow . . . is food tasting. We are **selecting** our menu for the four- to six-month flight that I will have in space. What is different about my next mission on the space station is that we will have a mixture of American and Russian food, so that will certainly make it different. . . . Perhaps I can come to your school someday and perhaps in fifteen years or so you can go to space!

Gary TX: What kind of work do you do when you are at the space station?

Dan Bursch: We have a crew of three— myself, Carl Walz (another American astronaut), and Yuri. He is a Russian **cosmonaut**. He will be our **commander**. We divide up the work because there is a lot of work to be done. . . .

---

chatted, talked informally

selecting, choosing
cosmonaut, Russian word for astronaut
commander, leader

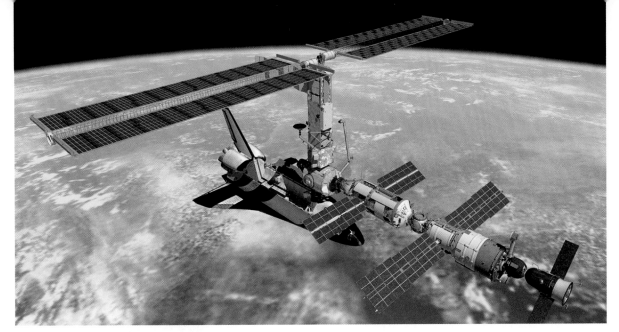

▲ The International Space Station

Galileo Guest: How do the astronauts deal with the effects of zero gravity on the space station?

Dan Bursch: Learning to work in space without feeling gravity is always a challenge. . . . Getting used to not feeling gravity usually takes a day or two.

International: What is it like working with scientists and other astronauts from all around the world? Do you all **get along**? Do you have fun?

Dan Bursch: This job is particularly interesting just because of that fact. . . . In the astronaut office, the range of different kinds of people is pretty wide. . . . But we all share one common goal, and that is to fly and live and work in space. . . .

Hollifeld: Can you see the lights of the world's cities from space?

---

get along, act friendly

Dan Bursch: Yes. We spend half of our time while **in orbit** on the dark side of the planet. If there is a thin cloud layer, you see kind of a glow like from a lampshade that dampens the light a little bit. But when it is clear—when there are no clouds—the lights are **spectacular.** . . .

Venus: What is the first time you go into space like? Is it hard to learn to use the tools or get used to things **floating around**?

---

in orbit, circling around Earth
spectacular, wonderful and exciting
floating around, moving around freely in the air

BEFORE YOU GO ON . . .

1 What is different about the menu on this trip?

2 What is a common goal for Bursch and the people he works with?

HOW ABOUT YOU?

• Would you like to live and work on the space station? Why or why not?

Dan Bursch: I remember my first flight in 1993 on [the space shuttle] *Discovery*. . . . At lift-off, there is a lot of vibration and a lot of noise, and eight-and-a-half minutes later you are in orbit. When the engines turn off, instantly everything floats. . . . You have to make sure that you either strap something down or use **Velcro** because you will probably lose it otherwise.

Fun 2 Travl: What are the **entertainment options** available to you during your **down time** on the space station?

Dan Bursch: We will have movies that we will be able to play in orbit. . . . People will try to bring up a **hobby** such as reading. . . . We do have e-mail. Most of our down time will be spent sending e-mails to our families and friends.

Jurgen: What kind of personal items will you take with you from Earth?

Dan Bursch: The most popular personal item is probably pictures of our families. Other things may include perhaps a special **memento**, either from a parent or a grandparent. But the most popular personal items are pictures. And usually ones that include some scene or the background of what it is like back on Earth.

AstroBob: Do you think that at some point ordinary people will get to go to the space station? Or will it always be **reserved for** scientists?

Dan Bursch: I think that is certainly a goal that we should try to reach. If it will be in my lifetime, I don't know. . . . When airplanes first came out, they were reserved at first for just the very **daring** or risk takers. And now anybody can fly on an airplane. So, I don't think it is a question of IF the opportunity will come . . . it is simply a matter of WHEN.

Sandy Fay: What kinds of things do they hope the space station will be good for once it is completed?

Dan Bursch: . . . I see the biggest challenge and the biggest thing that we are learning is two former enemies learning how to work together and build such a large and **complex** structure in space. And not just two former enemies, but all of the over one dozen countries that are working together. . . .

Discovery.com: Thank you, Dan, for chatting with us tonight.

---

reserved for, set aside for
daring, brave
complex, not simple; complicated

Velcro, a material made of two special pieces of cloth, used for fastening clothes, shoes, etc.
entertainment options, things to do for fun
down time, free time
hobby, something people do for pleasure during free time
memento, an item that helps you remember something or someone; a souvenir

BEFORE YOU GO ON . . .

1 What do astronauts bring with them to remind them of home?

2 For Dan Bursch, what is the biggest challenge of the space station?

HOW ABOUT YOU?
- What question would you like to ask Dan Bursch?

Link the Readings

Reread "Interview with an Astronaut." Then copy the chart into your notebook and complete it.

Title of Selection	Type of Text (Genre)	Fiction or Nonfiction	Purpose of Selection	How Travel Will Be Different in the Future
"Life in the Future"		*nonfiction*		
"Interview with an Astronaut: Dan Bursch"	*interview*			*Ordinary people will fly in space shuttles.*

DISCUSSION

Discuss in pairs or small groups.

1. Imagine you are going to the International Space Station. What personal items will you take with you?

2. Do you think humans will be able to live in space for a long time? Why or why not?

3. Dan Bursch talks about the challenges of living on the space station, such as choosing food, dealing with gravity, and working with others. What do you think would be your biggest challenge? Why?

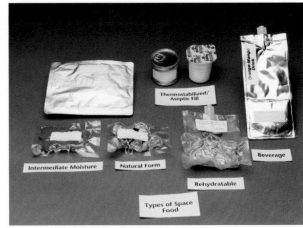

▲ Space food

Connect to Writing

GRAMMAR

Using *will* for the Future

Use ***will* + base form of the verb** to talk about the future. When you make predictions about the future, you use *will*.

> Astronauts **will fly** to Mars by the end of the century.
> Cars **will drive** themselves on automated highways.
> The population **will grow** to 11 billion by 2100.

Note that *will* is usually contracted to *'ll* in speaking and informal writing. Do not use contractions in formal writing.

> We**'ll build** a space station in ten years.

The contracted form of *will* + *not* is ***won't***.

> They probably **won't find** life on Mars.

Practice

Write sentences in your notebook. Use the words below to make predictions about the future.

Example: People (live) on space stations.
    People will live on space stations.

1. Fire-fighting robots (rescue) people.
2. In 2050 the population (be) 10 billion.
3. Humans (travel) to Mars.
4. Medical discoveries (help) people live longer.
5. Apartment buildings (have) 180 floors.
6. High-speed elevators (carry) eighty people at a time.
7. Cars (steer) themselves on automated highways.
8. Car manufacturers (make) safer, faster cars.
9. The price (be) $60,000.
10. People (fly) with jetpacks.

SKILLS FOR WRITING

Writing Notes for a Research Report

A research report gives detailed information about a topic. A writer can find facts about the topic in reference books, magazines, newspapers, and on the Internet. These are called sources. It is important to keep the facts from your sources organized. Before writers start writing a research report, they often organize facts by taking notes about each piece of information they find.

Here is an example of a note card for a research report on future transport. It is about one subtopic, or smaller topic, that the writer wants to include in the report.

NOTE-TAKING TIPS

- Use one note card for each subtopic.
- Summarize facts with your own words or phrases. Don't copy facts word for word from the source.
- For each note, record the source (the Internet, a book, a magazine, etc.). If the source is from the Internet, record the website address. If the source is a book, record the title, author, publisher, place and date of publication, and page number. For example, *Future*, by Michael Tambini, Dorling Kindersley, New York, 1998, p. 44.

Skycar M400

- *Paul Moller is developing a flying car called Skycar M400.*
- *Computers will control the car.*
- *Moller thinks Skycar will be the first mass-produced flying car.*
- *The first Skycar will cost about $1 million.*
- *Moller thinks it will cost about $60,000 to mass produce his car.*

Source: www.moller.com/skycar/

---

1. What subtopic is this note card about?
2. What source did the writer use for the notes on this card?
3. Where does the writer list the source?

WRITING ASSIGNMENT

Notes

You will research and take notes on a topic about the future that interests you.

1. **Read** Reread the note card on page 239. Then think of a topic you would like to write about, such as the growing population, future cities, future transport (cars, planes, and jetpacks), or future exploration.

Writing Strategy: Subtopic Web

After you choose a topic to research, you need to decide what subtopics you want to take notes on. Write your topic in the middle of a page and then brainstorm smaller topics that are related to your topic. Look at this subtopic web about future transport.

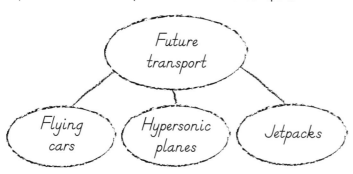

Narrow your ideas down to two subtopics. As you look at different sources, see which subtopics have the most information written about them. Choose two of these subtopics to write about.

1. Can you think of any other subtopics about future transport?
2. What sources can you check to get information about future transport?

---

2. **Make a subtopic web** Once you decide on a topic, make a subtopic web in your notebook. List as many subtopics as you can. Then narrow your list down to two or three subtopics.

3. **Write** Write one note card for each subtopic. Use only nonfiction sources that tell facts about your subtopics. Remember the rules for writing note cards.

EDITING CHECKLIST
Did you . . .

▶ look for facts about at least two subtopics?

▶ use your own words in your notes?

▶ record the source on each note card?

Check Your Knowledge

Language Development

1. Why do you summarize a text? Describe how you summarize.
2. Why do writers take notes?
3. What is a research report?
4. What is a subtopic? A subtopic web?
5. What are two sources of information that you can use when you are writing a research report?
6. Make three predictions about the future, using *will*.

Academic Content

1. What new social studies vocabulary did you learn in Part 1? What do the words mean?
2. What can a hypersonic plane do that a regular airplane cannot?
3. What are some differences between Earth and Mars?

Prepare to Read

OBJECTIVES

LANGUAGE DEVELOPMENT

Reading:
- Vocabulary building: *Context, dictionary skills*
- Reading strategy: *Reading for enjoyment*
- Text types: *Novel, science article*
- Literary element: *Dialogue*

Writing:
- Sentence outline
- Research report

Listening/Speaking:
- Listen to a report
- Present a report

Grammar:
- Future: *be going to*

Viewing/Representing:
- Inherited traits

ACADEMIC CONTENT
- Science vocabulary
- DNA, genes, and traits
- Make predictions about life in the future

BACKGROUND

The Time Warp Trio: 2095 is a science fiction story about traveling into the future. Science fiction combines elements of fiction and fantasy with scientific fact. Most science fiction stories are set in the future. In this excerpt, the characters travel into the future, to the year 2095.

Make connections Pretend that you are able to travel 100 years into the future. Copy this chart into your notebook. Fill in the blanks with predictions of how people, places, and things will look.

People, Places, or Things	What They Will Look Like in the Future
My home	
My school	
My town	
My family	

▲ An artist's idea of a city of the future

LEARN KEY WORDS

mechanical
plastic
revolutionary
stories
streamlined
transported

VOCABULARY

Read these sentences. Use the context to figure out the meaning of the **red** words. Use a dictionary to check your answers. Write each word and its meaning in your notebook.

1. The **mechanical** sidewalk moves people quickly from place to place.
2. Her **plastic** raincoat kept her dry in the rain.
3. The new invention was **revolutionary**—it changed the way that people lived.
4. The tall buildings had 200 **stories**! We couldn't see the top.
5. Cars of the future will be smaller, faster, and more **streamlined** than cars of the past.
6. They pressed the numbers and were **transported** 100 years into the future.

READING STRATEGY

Reading for Enjoyment

Sometimes you read for information. Other times you read just for fun or entertainment. When your purpose for reading is to enjoy, you want to be entertained by the characters, the setting, and the pictures that go with the text. People often read novels to be entertained.

Think about how the words and pictures in this excerpt make you want to read more.

Novel

Read this science fiction novel excerpt for your enjoyment. Are the characters, the setting, and the story entertaining? Why or why not?

from

THE TIME WARP TRIO: 2095

Jon Scieszka

Sam, Fred, and Joe are a trio, or three friends. They are visiting the American Museum of Natural History in New York City in the year 1995. Joe, the narrator, has The Book, *a time-travel guide given to him by his Uncle Joe. Without meaning to, Joe does something that transports him and his two friends into the year 2095. As this excerpt begins, the trio is running away from a security robot a called a SellBot.*

We jumped over the twitching SellBot and ran down a **flight of stairs**. We had almost made it to the lobby, when the sound of a buzzer filled the halls.

The museum doors opened. A **tidal wave of people** came flooding in, and we were right in its path.

We dodged the first bunch of teenagers. They had corkscrew, spike, and Mohawk hair in every color you can think of. But the most amazing thing was that no one was touching the ground.

"They're flying. People in the future have figured out how to fly," said Sam.

A solid river of people flowed past us. An old man in an aluminum suit. A woman with leopard-patterned skin. A class in shiny school uniforms. Everyone was floating about a foot above the floor.

"How do they do that?" I said.

LITERARY ELEMENT

Dialogue is what characters say to each other. The words in quotation marks (" ") tell the exact words of the characters.

---

flight of stairs, steps from one floor to the next
tidal wave of people, a large crowd of people

"Look closely," said Sam. "Everyone has a small disk with a green triangle and a red square."

"Hey, you're right," I said.

"I'm always right," said Sam. "That is obviously the **antigravity disk** that kid was talking about. Now let's get out of here before another SellBot **tracks us down**."

Fred grabbed my belt. Sam grabbed Fred's belt. And we fought our way outside. We stopped at the statue of Teddy Roosevelt sitting on his horse looking out over Central Park. We stood and looked out with him.

"Wow," said Fred. "I see it but I don't believe it."

The sidewalk was full of floating people of every shape and color. There were people with green skin, blue skin, purple skin, orange, striped, plaid, dotted, and **you-name-it skin**. The street was packed three high and three deep with floating bullet-shaped things that must have been antigravity cars. And all around the trees of Central Park, towering buildings spread up and out like gigantic mechanical trees taller than the clouds.

---

antigravity disk, a small item that fights the force of gravity, allowing one to float above the ground
tracks us down, finds us
you-name-it skin, every kind of skin

BEFORE YOU GO ON . . .

1. Where are the boys transported?

2. What is New York like in the future?

HOW ABOUT YOU?
- Imagine that you could travel to any time period. Which would you choose?

Layers and layers of antigravity cars and lines of people snaked around a hundred stories above us. New York was bigger, busier, and noisier than ever. . . .

* * *

Now wearing antigravity disks, the boys fly through the streets of New York, still chased by the SellBot and three futuristic girls who look strangely familiar. Uncle Joe has appeared out of nowhere to help. The girls catch up, and Joe is surprised to see that one of the girls looks very much like his sister.

"Come on," said the girl who looked like my sister. "Follow us."

Sam looked at Fred. Fred looked at me. I looked at Uncle Joe.

"Do we have any choice?" I asked.

We **took off** and followed the girls around the buildings, over crowds of crazily colored people, past streamlined **pods** and more talking, blinking, singing 3-D ads, until I had no idea where we were.

We finally stopped in front of a building too tall to believe.

"Here's my house," said the **lead girl**.

Fred, Sam, and I looked up and up and up at the building that disappeared in the clouds.

The girl led us through a triangle door that opened at her voice. She put her hand over a blinking red handprint on the wall. And in five seconds we were all transported to a room that must have been five miles above New York City.

___

took off, left quickly
pods, long vehicles
lead girl, girl at the front of the others

The girls flopped down on cushions. "This is my room," said the girl who looked like my sister.

We stood nervously in one corner.

"So you're not **killer time cops**?" I said.

The three girls looked at me like I was crazy.

"Of course not," said one.

"Whatever gave you that idea?" said another.

Then we all started asking questions.

___

killer time cops, secret police who catch time travelers

"Who are you guys?"

"How did you know we'd be at the museum?"

"Do you have anything to eat?"

The girls laughed. The one who led us there pushed a green dot on a small table. A bowl of something looking like dried green dog food appeared with a pile of liquid filled plastic balls.

"Here's some **Vitagorp and Unicola**," said the girl who looked like my sister. "Now let me try to explain things from the beginning."

We copied the girls and sucked on the plastic ball things the same way they did. Fred ate a handful of the green dog food.

"I'm Joanie. This is Samantha. That's Frieda."

"But everybody calls me Freddi," said the girl with the baseball hat.

"And we have these names," Joanie continued, "because we were named after our great-grandfathers—Joe, Sam, and Fred."

"Or in other words—you," said Samantha.

Everything suddenly made sense. That's why they looked so much like us.

"Of course," said Uncle Joe, dusting off his **top hat**. "Your great-grandkids have to make sure you get back to 1995. Otherwise you won't have kids. Then your kids won't have kids. Then your kids' kids won't have—"

Vitagorp and Unicola, imaginary food and drink of the future
top hat, tall black hat

"Us," said Samantha. "Your great-grandkids. And we knew you would be at the museum because you wrote us a note." Samantha handed me a yellowed sheet of paper that had been sealed in plastic. It was our Museum Worksheet from 1995. On the back was a note in my handwriting that said:

Girls,
Meet us under Teddy Roosevelt's statue at the Museum of Natural History, September 28, 2095.
Sincerely,
Joe, Sam, Fred

"How did you get our worksheet from 1995?" asked Sam.

"I got it from my mom," said Joanie. "And she got it from her mom."

"But we didn't write that," I said.

"You will," said Samantha, "if we can get you back to 1995."

BEFORE YOU GO ON . . .

1 Who are the three girls?

2 How do the girls know the boys will be at the museum?

HOW ABOUT YOU?

- Imagine you are Joe. How do you feel at this point in the story?

247

"Saved by our own great-grandkids with a note we haven't written yet?" said Sam. "I told you something like this was going to happen. Now we're probably going to **blow up** ."

"Wow," said Fred, eating more Vitagorp. "Our own great-grandkids. So what team is that on your hat? I've never seen that **logo** ."

"That's the **Yankees** ," said Freddi. "They changed it when Grandma was **pitching** ."

"Your grandma? Fred's daughter?" I said. "A pitcher for the Yankees?"

"Not just a pitcher. She was a great pitcher," said Freddi. "2.79 lifetime ERA, 275 wins, 3 no-hitters, and the Cy Young award in '37."*

"Forget your granny's **stats** ," said Sam. "We could be genius inventors back in 1995 if we could reconstruct these **levitation devices** ."

"What did he just say?" asked Freddi.

"He wants to know how the antigravity disks work," said Samantha. "A truly amazing discovery. More surprising than Charles Goodyear's accidental discovery of vulcanized rubber. More revolutionary than Alexander Graham Bell's first telephone. But all I can tell you is that the antigravity power comes from the chemical BHT. And it was discovered in a breakfast accident."

"What's a breakfast accident?" said Sam. "A **head-on collision** with a bowl of cornflakes? And who found out BHT could make things fly?"

"You did," said Samantha. "That's why we can't tell you more. You know the Time Warp Info-Speed Limit posted in *The Book*. Anyone traveling through time with too much information from another time blows up."

Sam's eyes nearly **bugged out** of his head. "I knew it. Don't tell me another word."

"Hey, wait a minute," I said. "Where did you say that info-speed limit was?"

Samantha looked at me like I was an insect.

"In *The Book*, of course."

"How do you know about *The Book*?"

"I got it for my birthday last year," said Joanie.

"And since then we've been all over time," said Freddi. "We've met cavewomen, Ann the Pirate, **Calamity Jane** . . . ."

"And don't forget **Cleopatra** and the underground cities of Venus," said Samantha.

"But if you have *The Book*, that means we're saved," said Sam.

---

* This information shows that Fred's future daughter is a great baseball player. This is especially interesting because there are no women players in professional baseball today.

---

blow up, explode and die
logo, brand name or label
Yankees, New York baseball team
pitching, throwing a ball to a batter
stats, short for statistics—facts about a certain subject
levitation devices, machines that let you float off the ground

head-on collision, a violent crash
bugged out, popped out
Calamity Jane, American frontier woman from the 1800s famous for her unconventional behavior and courage
Cleopatra, ancient Egyptian queen

Samantha gave Sam her look. "If you remember the Time Warpers' Tips, you know nothing can be in two places at once. Of course our *Book* disappeared as soon as your *Book* appeared."

"So now we have to help you get *The Book* back to the past," said Freddi, "so we can have it in the future."

"Of course," said Sam.

"We knew that," said Fred.

"Uh, right . . ." I said, trying to talk my way out of this mess. "We knew that would happen, but we uh . . . " I looked around at Sam, Fred, Samantha, Freddi, and Joanie. Then I **spotted** Uncle Joe. "We thought we could really learn some tricks about finding *The Book* from Uncle Joe!"

Uncle Joe looked up from something he was **fiddling with** in his lap. "*The Book*? Oh, I never could get it to work the way your mother did. That's why I gave it to you for your birthday."

"Oh, great," said Sam. "We're **doomed**."

---

spotted, saw
fiddling with, playing with
doomed, in a hopeless situation

"But that's also why I put this together." Uncle Joe held up the thing he had been fiddling with in his lap. It was an old-fashioned pocket watch. "My Time Warp Watch."

"We're saved!" yelled Sam.

About the Author

Jon Scieszka

Jon Scieszka has written many books for kids. Other books in the Time Warp Trio series include *The Good, the Bad, and the Goofy; Knights of the Kitchen Table; The Not-So-Jolly Roger;* and *Your Mother Was a Neanderthal.*

BEFORE YOU GO ON . . .

1. Which character discovered the antigravity disk, but doesn't know it?
2. What will happen to the boys if they learn too much information while visiting the future?

HOW ABOUT YOU?

- Imagine you are able to travel through time. Who would you take with you? Why?

249

Review and Practice

Reread the excerpt from *The Time Warp Trio: 2095.* Then copy the chart into your notebook and complete it. In the right column, write sentences telling what you enjoyed in the story.

	What I Enjoyed
Characters	
Pictures	
Setting	
Details about Everyday Life in the Future	

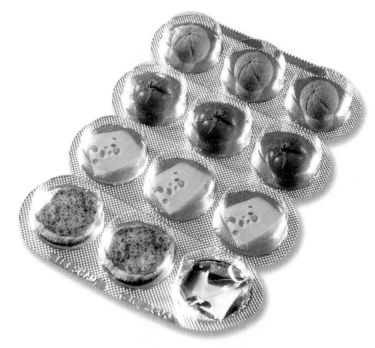

▲ How future food may look

EXTENSION

1. The girls offer the boys Vitagorp and Unicola. Make up your own food of the future. What does it look and smell like? What is its name?

2. Create an advertisement for a food or another product for 2095. Draw a picture of the product and write a description of it.

3. Make a TV commercial for your product. Practice your commercial and perform it for the class.

DISCUSSION

Discuss in pairs or small groups.

1. What do you think was the best part of time travel for Sam, Fred, and Joe? What was the worst part?

2. How did the dialogue in the excerpt from *The Time Warp Trio: 2095* help you understand the characters?

3. Reread the definition of "science fiction" on page 242. Can you find some fiction, some fantasy, and some scientific fact in *The Time Warp Trio: 2095*? Explain.

An artist's idea of a city of the future ▶

This is a science article. You will read facts about DNA—the "building blocks" of all forms of life. The purpose of this article is to give information about DNA. After each section, stop and summarize what you read.

DNA, Genes, and Traits

What Is DNA?

Every form of life is put together and controlled by a chemical "recipe," or code, called DNA (**d**eoxyribo**n**ucleic **a**cid). DNA is found in cells—very small parts of humans, animals, and plants. DNA contains genes. Genes on DNA look something like a supermarket **bar code**. The white lines are DNA. The black lines are genes. The code determines the **characteristics** of every living thing.

What Are Genes?

Each human cell contains 50,000 to 100,000 small parts called genes. Each gene controls a different trait, such as eye color or height. Genes get passed on from **generation** to generation. A baby **inherits** half its genes from its mother and half from its father. So, a baby inherits a quarter of its genes from each grandmother and a quarter from each grandfather.

Genes and People

Unless you are an identical twin, you are unique. This means that nobody else has exactly the same genes as you, not even your brothers and sisters.

Genes control all your traits. One gene controls skin color. Three genes control eye color.

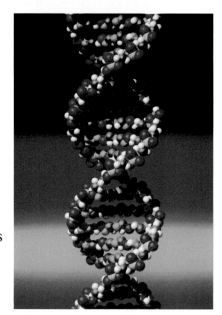

▲ A model of DNA that is found in cells

▲ Identical twins share the same genes.

---

bar code, a group of thin and thick lines on a product, which a computer in a store reads to find the price
characteristics, traits; qualities
generation, all the people who are about the same age in a family
inherits, gets; receives

How Traits Are Inherited

Children often look like their parents in some ways. They can also look like their aunts or uncles, their grandparents, and their great-grandparents. The following traits are often inherited:

- eye color
- hair color
- dimples
- widow's peak
- cleft chin

Dimples are small hollows in the skin. Some people get them around their mouth when they smile. A cleft chin is a dimple in the chin. A hairline that comes to a point in the middle of your forehead is called a widow's peak.

BEFORE YOU GO ON . . .

1 Where is DNA found?

2 What are some traits that people inherit?

HOW ABOUT YOU?

- Name two traits you or someone you know inherited from a parent or grandparent.

GRACIELA SEGOVIA'S FAMILY

Fernando   Jimena   Pedro   Teresa

Luz   Alvaro   Elena   Mario

Graciela

▲ This family tree shows how family members share traits.

DNA and Solving Crimes

Forensic scientists are people who study crimes by looking at **evidence**. Many forensic scientists use scientific or medical tests to solve crimes. One test is for DNA. A sample of blood, hair, or other body **tissue** found at the scene of a crime is tested. The DNA from the sample can be matched to a suspect's DNA to find out if he or she **committed the crime**.

▲ A scientist studies a DNA sequence.

In recent years, many people have been released from prison after DNA tests proved that they were **innocent**. Law students at the Wisconsin Innocence Project **investigate** about twenty to thirty criminal cases at any given time. In 2001, the project was responsible for the release of a Texas prisoner, Chris Ochoa. He was serving a life sentence for a 1988 murder. DNA tests on samples found on the victim proved that Ochoa did not commit the crime. He was innocent. Chris Ochoa spent twelve years in prison for a crime he didn't commit.

▲ Chris Ochoa and the students who helped to free him

DNA testing is now a very important tool in criminal investigation, and it is going to be more important in the future. More forensic scientists are going to use DNA tests to help make sure the right people are punished for their crimes.

---

evidence, proof
tissue, material from the body, such as skin and muscle
committed the crime, did something wrong or illegal
innocent, not guilty
investigate, look into; research

BEFORE YOU GO ON . . .

1 What can scientists test to find DNA?

2 How did DNA testing help Chris Ochoa?

HOW ABOUT YOU?
- Would you like to be a forensic scientist? Why or why not?

Link the Readings

REFLECTION

Reread "DNA, Genes, and Traits" and think about the excerpt from *The Time Warp Trio: 2095*. Then copy the chart into your notebook and complete it.

Title of Selection	Type of Text (Genre)	Fiction or Nonfiction	Purpose of Selection	Invention That Helps People
From *The Time Warp Trio: 2095*			*to entertain*	
"DNA, Genes, and Traits"	*science article*			

DISCUSSION

Discuss in pairs or small groups.

1. One of the girls in 2095 looks very much like Joe's sister. Why is this fact important?

2. Everyone has his or her own special code called DNA. How is this fact important in *The Time Warp Trio: 2095* excerpt? How is it important in real life?

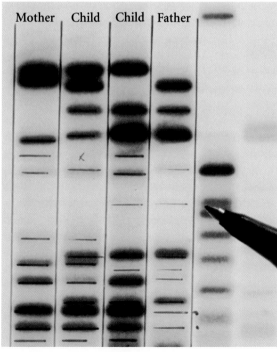

▲ The bands in these DNA sequences show that both children share some bands with each parent, proving that they are related.

Connect to Writing

GRAMMAR

Using *be going to* for the Future
Use ***be going to* + base form of the verb** to talk about future plans.

> I**'m going to visit** my grandparents this weekend.
> My parents **are going to talk** to my teacher tonight.

Will and *be going to* have the same meaning when making predictions about the future.

> Forensic scientists **will help** solve more crimes using DNA tests.
> Forensic scientists **are going to help** solve more crimes using DNA tests.

Practice

Write sentences in your notebook using the words below and a form of *be going to*.

Example: Helen (visit me) on Friday.
      Helen is going to visit me on Friday.

1. My sister (call) home this evening.
2. Joanie, Freddi, and Samantha (buy) new antigravity disks next week.
3. I (see) the doctor tomorrow morning.
4. We (watch) my sister play tennis after school.
5. He (stay) home tonight.
6. My grandfather (fix) his car this weekend.
7. Forensic scientists (do) more DNA tests in the future.
8. Ricardo and Luz (travel) in Mexico this summer.
9. Joe (buy) a computer next month.
10. "We're (blow up)," said Sam.

SKILLS FOR WRITING

Making Sentence Outlines

The first and second steps in writing a research report are choosing a topic and researching it. The third step is organizing the facts you found in your research in an outline. One type of outline is called a sentence outline. In a sentence outline, you group facts together under main ideas and supporting ideas.

Look at this sentence outline about the Skycar M400. Then answer the questions.

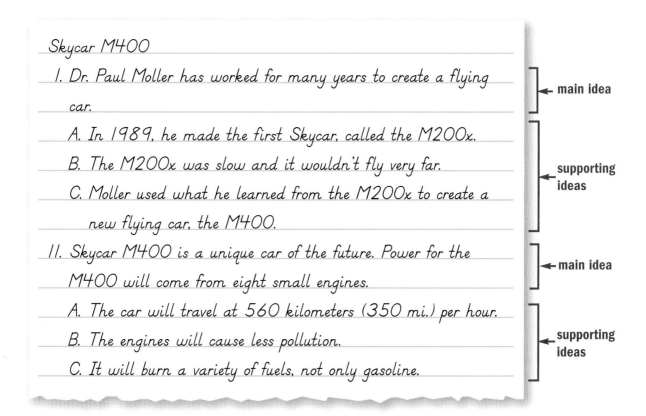

Skycar M400

I. Dr. Paul Moller has worked for many years to create a flying car. ← main idea

  A. In 1989, he made the first Skycar, called the M200x.

  B. The M200x was slow and it wouldn't fly very far.

  C. Moller used what he learned from the M200x to create a new flying car, the M400. ← supporting ideas

II. Skycar M400 is a unique car of the future. Power for the M400 will come from eight small engines. ← main idea

  A. The car will travel at 560 kilometers (350 mi.) per hour.

  B. The engines will cause less pollution.

  C. It will burn a variety of fuels, not only gasoline. ← supporting ideas

1. What is the first main idea?
2. Do the sentences under it support it?
3. What is the second main idea?
4. Do the sentences under it support it?

WRITING ASSIGNMENT

Sentence Outlines

You will make a sentence outline of the text "DNA, Genes, and Traits" on pages 252–254.

1. **Read** Reread the sentence outline on page 257. Note how the writer used main ideas and supporting ideas.

Writing Strategy: Outline

Follow this outline to organize the information in the article. Try to have at least two supporting details under each main idea. This will help you know whether you need to find more information about your topic.

Outline

I. Main Idea
   A. Supporting Detail
   B. Supporting Detail
   C. Supporting Detail
II. Main Idea
   A. Supporting Detail
   B. Supporting Detail
III. Main Idea
   A. Supporting Detail
   B. Supporting Detail

1. How many main ideas are there in this research report?
2. How many supporting details are there about the first main idea?

---

2. **Make an outline** Use the sentence outline on page 257 and the outline above as models. Start your outline by filling in the main ideas from the article "DNA, Genes, and Traits." The headings can be the main ideas for your outline.

3. **Write** Write supporting ideas under each main idea in your outline. How many main ideas do you have?

EDITING CHECKLIST

Did you . . .

▶ list the main ideas first?
▶ find at least two supporting details for each main idea?
▶ remember to indent the details?
▶ use any sentences in the future?

Check Your Knowledge

Language Development

1. How did your purpose differ in reading the excerpt from *The Time Warp Trio: 2095* and "DNA, Genes, and Traits"?

2. What is dialogue? What are quotation marks? Give examples.

3. What is science fiction? Why is *The Time Warp Trio: 2095* science fiction?

4. What is the reason to make a sentence outline when you write a report?

5. What information is included in an outline?

6. Give an example of *be going to* to talk about future plans.

Academic Content

1. What new science vocabulary did you learn in Part 2? What do the words mean?

2. What do you call the chemical code found in every cell?

3. Where are genes located and what do they do?

4. How do forensic scientists use DNA to help solve crimes?

Put It All Together

OBJECTIVES

Integrate Skills
- Listening/ Speaking: *Presentation*
- Writing: *Research report*

Investigate Themes
- Projects
- Further reading

LISTENING and SPEAKING WORKSHOP

PRESENTATION

You will give a presentation on an invention that will help students in the future.

1 **Think about it** Think about inventions that help you now, such as computers and calculators. What inventions would help students in the future? Write some ideas for future machines that would help you in school.

Work in small groups. Compare and discuss your ideas for future inventions. Choose one invention that you all think would help many students.

2 **Organize** Choose one group member to present the report to the class. Work together to write a description of your invention. Make a large drawing of the invention that the speaker can point to as he or she is talking. Make note cards that the speaker can look at while describing the invention.

3 **Practice** Listen carefully to your group speaker as he or she practices presenting the report. Make suggestions on how to make the presentation better.

4 **Present and evaluate** Present your group's report to the class. Then invite students to ask questions about the invention. After each speaker finishes, evaluate the presentation. Was each speaker's explanation and drawing clear? Do you have any suggestions for improvement?

SPEAKING TIPS

- Stand up straight, and speak loudly and clearly. Try to speak slowly.
- Point to your drawing to emphasize important information.
- Make eye contact with your classmates. Talk to your audience, not to your drawing.

LISTENING TIP

As you listen to a report, review in your mind the speaker's main ideas. This helps you pay attention to the speaker and to remember the important points.

260

RESEARCH REPORT

In a research report, the writer gathers and presents information about a topic from different sources, such as reference books, the Internet, and interviews. The writer's purpose is to explain a topic or to answer a question about it.

A good research report includes the following characteristics:

- a topic or question that the writer investigates and explains

- a main idea that gives the writer's purpose for the research report

- information about the topic from different sources, stated in the writer's own words

- clearly organized facts that explain the topic and support the writer's main ideas

- a list of the writer's sources

You will write a three-paragraph research report on a topic about the future. Research one of the topics from the list below, or choose another topic that interests you.

DNA Testing	Future Travel
Cars of the Future	Robots
Space Stations	Future Entertainment
A Space Colony	Cities of the Future
Computers	Future Schools

1 **Prewrite** Look up the topic in reference books and on the Internet to find information. Next, take notes about the topic and subtopics. Write them on note cards. If necessary, reread how to take notes in Skills for Writing on page 239. Then organize your note cards by main ideas. Write a sentence outline for your research report. Review how to write a sentence outline in Skills for Writing on page 257.

WRITING TIP

As you do research, narrow your topic. For example, the topic "Cars of the Future" is too broad because there are too many different kinds of cars. To narrow your topic, ask yourself questions such as "What are the characteristics of one future car?" or "What makes this future car unique?" The answers to these questions will help you choose the main idea of your report.

Before you write a first draft of your report, read the following model. Notice the characteristics of a research report.

Thomas José Harding

Skycar M400: Car of the Future

Dr. Paul Moller has a dream: to design, manufacture, and sell a flying car. In 1989, his company made a flying car called Skycar M200x. The M200x was slow and didn't fly very far. Dr. Moller then developed the Skycar M400. He believes that it will be the car of the future.

Skycar M400 is going to have some amazing features. It will take off and land like a helicopter. Skycar M400 will travel at a top speed of 560 kilometers (350 mi.) per hour and will get about 32 kilometers (20 mi.) to a gallon of gasoline.

The first M400 cars will have human pilots, but later models will be computer-driven. The first Skycar M400 will cost about $1 million, but Dr. Moller believes it will cost only about $60,000 to mass produce the car.

Sources:

www.moller.com/skycar/

Future, by Michael Tambini, Dorling Kindersley, New York, 1998

www.howstuffworks.com/flying-car2.htm

The writer has narrowed his topic to a specific car.

He clearly states the main idea of his report.

He includes facts to explain and support his main idea.

He includes information from several sources and lists the sources.

2 **Draft** Use your sentence outline and the model to write your research report.

3 **Edit** Work in pairs. Trade reports. Use the editing checklist to evaluate each other's writing.

> ## EDITING CHECKLIST
> ### Did you . . .
> ▶ narrow your research to a specific topic or question?
> ▶ state the main idea of your research?
> ▶ include information from several sources?
> ▶ state information in your own words?
> ▶ organize your report clearly, using two or three main ideas?
> ▶ include a list of your sources?
> ▶ use correct grammar and punctuation?

4 **Revise** Revise your report. Add or rearrange information to make your report easier to read and understand.

5 **Publish** Share your research report with your teacher and your classmates. If possible, show pictures that illustrate your topic and any important person or people connected to the topic.

▲ A solar-powered car of the future

PROJECTS

Work in pairs or small groups. Choose one of these projects.

1 With your group, talk about ideas for a science fiction story. What would be a good time period for the story? What scientific facts do you want to include? What are some things that will happen? Then draft your story. Include some dialogue.

2 Find out more information about the inventions listed on the timeline on page 226. Look for facts in magazines, reference books, and on the Internet. Make a visual aid about the invention you research and share your information with the class.

3 Paint or draw a picture of what you think certain people, places, or objects might look like 100 years from now. Create an art gallery of the future in the classroom to display the pictures.

4 With a family member, look through old and current photo albums. Discuss traits that have been passed on to several members of your family like hair or eye color. Look for features that are unique to your family.

5 Invite a forensic scientist to speak to the class about tools that are used to gather and test evidence. Before the person comes, brainstorm questions to ask him or her after the talk.

6 Create a comic strip about characters who live in the future. Show what they look like, where they live, and how they travel. You can make your comic strip funny or serious. Place the comic strips together in a class comic book.

▲ The Hamm family of Dallas, Texas, includes five sets of twins and one "single" child.

Further Reading

To find out more about the theme of this unit, choose from these reading suggestions.

Robotz, **Stephen Munzer** This encyclopedia of robots in fact and fiction covers robots past, present, and future. You'll get tips on building your own robots, learn about artificial intelligence, and be treated to a glimpse of future robots.

The New Way Things Work, **David Macaulay** This beautifully illustrated book contains a wealth of information about how things work, from everyday items, such as keys and can openers, to the most complex, including compact disks, computer hard drives, and the Internet. The explanations are easy to understand and fun to read.

Outernet: Friend or Foe?, **Steve Barlow and Steve Skidmore** It all started with a birthday present—what appeared to be a laptop computer. But Jack, Loaf, and Merle are about to discover that this laptop is much more than they imagined. They accidentally connect to an intergalactic Internet, called the Outernet, via a lost Server. There they encounter the evil Tyrant and his henchmen (the FOES) who are trying to take over the Outernet to use its powers to control the galaxy.

A Wrinkle in Time, **Madeleine L'Engle** In this story, Charles Wallace, Meg Murry, and their mother go off to rescue Meg and Charles Wallace's father, who mysteriously disappeared while he was experimenting with time travel. Their voyage takes them on an exciting trip through space, battling the forces of evil.

A Wind in the Door, **Madeleine L'Engle** Charles Wallace, Meg Murry's six-year-old brother, is very ill. To save him, Meg, Charles Wallace, and their friend Calvin O'Keefe go off on an extraordinary journey into galactic space—both fantastic and frightening—where they battle evil. This book is a companion to *A Wrinkle in Time.*

COMPARE AND CONTRAST
/kəm pâr′ and kən trast′ /
When you compare and contrast texts, you consider what is similar about the texts (compare) and what is different (contrast).

COMPOUND SENTENCE
/kom′pound sen′təns /
A compound sentence is made up of two simple sentences that are joined by a conjunction, such as *and, but,* and *or.*

CONJUNCTION /kən jungk′shən /
A conjunction connects words, groups of words, and sentences. The words *and, but, so,* and *or* are conjunctions.

CONTRACTION /kən trak′shən /
A contraction is a short form used to join two words together. For example, the contraction of *I am* (the verb *be* and the subject pronoun *I*) is *I'm.* The contraction of *you are* is *you're.* In a contraction, an apostrophe replaces one or more letters. Contractions are used in speaking and informal writing.

DIALOGUE /dī′ə lòg /
A dialogue is a conversation between characters. In novels, short stories, and poems, dialogue is usually shown by quotation marks to indicate a speaker's exact words. In a play, dialogue follows the names of characters, and no quotation marks are used.

DIARY /dī′ə rē /
A diary is a book in which you write each day about your personal thoughts, things that happened to you, or about things that you did.

DISTINGUISHING FACT AND OPINION
/dis ting′gwish ing fakt and ə pin′yən /
A fact is a statement someone can prove. An opinion is a belief that cannot be proved. Distinguishing fact and opinion means seeing the difference between what is a fact and what is an opinion in a text.

EXCERPT /ek′sėrpt′ /
An excerpt is a short passage or section taken from a longer text, such as a letter, a book, an article, a poem, a play, a speech, etc.

FABLE /fā′bəl /
A fable is a brief story or poem, usually with animal characters, that teaches a lesson, or moral. The moral is usually stated at the end of the fable.

FICTION /fik′shən /
Fiction is prose writing that tells about imaginary characters and events. Short stories and novels are works of fiction.

FLASHBACK /flash′bak′ /
A flashback is a scene within a story that interrupts the sequence of events to tell about something that happened in the past.

GENRE /jän′rə /
A genre is a division or type of literature. Literature is commonly divided into three major genres: poetry, prose (fiction and nonfiction), and drama (plays).

HISTORICAL FICTION
/hi stôr′ə kəl fik′shən /
Historical fiction, such as a historical novel, combines imaginary elements (fiction) with real people, events, or settings (history).

INFORMATIONAL TEXT
/in′fər mā′shən əl tekst/
An informational text is a nonfiction text. It is about real facts or events. The purpose of an informational text is to inform the reader about real facts, people, or events.

IMPERATIVE /im per′ə tiv/
An imperative is the form of a verb used for giving an instruction, a direction, or an order: *Give me the ball. Turn to the right. Come here!*

INTERVIEW /in′tər vyü/
An interview is an occasion when a famous person is asked questions about his or her life, opinions, etc.

LETTER /let′ər/
A letter is a written communication from one person to another. In personal letters, the writer shares information and his or her thoughts and feelings with one other person or group.

MAKING INFERENCES
/ma′king in′fər ans es/
Figuring out a writer's meaning when the writer suggests something rather than presenting information directly is called making an inference.

MOOD /müd/
Mood, or atmosphere, is the feeling created in the reader by a literary work or passage. The mood can be sad, funny, scary, tense, happy, hopeless, etc.

MYSTERY /mis′tər ē/
A mystery is something that is difficult to understand or explain. In a mystery story, the characters as well as the readers are given clues, or hints, to solve, or figure out, the mystery.

MYTH /mith/
A myth, like a fable, is a short fictional tale. Myths explain the actions of gods and heroes or the origins of elements of nature. Their purpose is to entertain and instruct. Every ancient culture has its collection of myths, or mythology, that is passed from parents to children as part of the "oral tradition."

NARRATIVE /nar′ə tiv/
A narrative is a story that can be either fiction or nonfiction. Novels and short stories are fictional narratives. Biographies and autobiographies are nonfiction narratives. In a personal narrative, the writer tells about something he or she experienced.

NARRATOR /nar′ā tər/
A narrator is a speaker or character who tells a story. The narrator sometimes takes part in the action while telling the story. Other times, the narrator is outside the action and just speaks about it.

NONFICTION /non fik′shən/
Nonfiction is prose writing that tells about real people, places, objects, or events. Biographies, reports, and newspaper articles are examples of nonfiction.

NOTING CAUSES AND EFFECTS
/nōt′ing kȯz′ əz and ə fekts′/
Noting causes and effects as you read can help you better understand a text. Most fiction and nonfiction texts tell about events. Why an event happens is a cause. What happens as a result of a cause is an effect. The words *so* and *because* often signal causes and effects.

Glossary

ACTIVE VOICE /akʹtiv vois/
A verb is in the active voice when its subject is the performer of the action: *The firefighters rescue people from the building.*

ADJECTIVE /ajʹik tiv/
An adjective describes nouns (people, places, animals, and things) or pronouns. In the sentence *I have a blue car*, the word *blue* is an adjective.

ADVERB /adʹvèrb/
An adverb usually describes the action of a verb, such as how an action happens: *The boy runs quickly.* The adverb *quickly* describes the verb *runs*. Several adverbs, such as *always, usually, often, sometimes,* and *never*, are called frequency adverbs: *She never found her necklace.*

ALLITERATION /ə litʹə rāʹshən/
Alliteration is the poetic use of two or more words that begin with the same sound. Writers use alliteration to draw attention to certain words or ideas, to imitate sounds, and to create musical effects.

ANALYZING HISTORICAL CONTEXT
/anʹə līz ing hi stôr ə kəl konʹtekst/
Sometimes the historical context, or the political and social events and trends of the time, plays a key role in a story setting. For example, in *The Diary of Anne Frank: The Play*, the historical context is the experience of the Jews in Holland during World War II. As you read, ask yourself what effect the historical setting has on the characters and the action. This will help you understand both the characters and the action better.

ARTICLE /ärʹtə kəl/
An article is a piece of nonfictional writing that is usually part of a newspaper or magazine.

AUTOBIOGRAPHY /ȯʹtə bī ogʹrə fē/
An autobiography is the story of the writer's own life, told by the writer, usually in the first person. It may tell about the person's whole life or only a part of it. Because autobiographies are about real people and events, they are nonfictional. Most autobiographies are written in the first person.

BASE FORM /bās fôrm/
The base form, or simple form, of a verb has no added ending (*-s, -ing, -ed*). *Talk* is the base form of the verb talk. (Other forms of *talk* are *talks, talking*, and *talked*.)

BIOGRAPHY /bī ogʹrə fē/
A biography is a nonfictional story of a person's life told by another person. Most biographies are written about famous or admirable people.

CHARACTER /karʹik tər/
A character is a person or an animal that takes part in the action of a literary work.

CHARACTERIZATION
/karʹik tər ə zāʹshən/
Characterization is the creation and development of a character in a story. Writers sometimes show what a character is like by describing what the character says and does.

COMPARATIVE /kəm parʹə tiv/
A comparative is an adjective or adverb used to compare two things. Most one-syllable adjectives and some two-syllable adjectives add *-er* for comparatives: *Bigger* is the comparative form of *big*. Most adjectives of two or more syllables use *more* for comparatives: *This rose is more fragrant than that one.* (*See also* Superlative.)

266

NOUN /noun/
A noun is the name of a person, thing, place, or animal. *Plane, building,* and *child* are common nouns. *Robert, Chicago,* and *Puerto Rico* are proper nouns.

NOVEL /nov′əl/
A novel is a long work of fiction. Novels contain such elements as characters, plot, conflict, and setting. The writer of novels develops these elements.

PASSIVE VOICE /pas′iv vois/
In the passive voice, the subject of the sentence receives the action: *The ball was caught by the outfielder.*

PERSONIFICATION
/pər son′ə fə kā′shən/
Personification is giving human traits to animals or inanimate objects.

PLAY /plā/
A play is a story performed by people in a theater.

PLAYWRIGHT /plā′rīt/
A playwright is a person who writes plays.

PLOT /plot/
A plot is a sequence of connected events in a fictional story. In most stories, the plot has characters and a main problem or conflict. After the problem is introduced, it grows until a turning point, or climax, when a character tries to solve the problem. The end of the story usually follows the climax.

POEM /pō′əm/
A poem is a piece of writing that uses a pattern of lines and sounds to express ideas, emotions, etc.

POINT OF VIEW /point ov vyü/
A narrator tells a story from his or her point of view. In the first-person point of view, the narrator tells the story using *I* and *my*. In the third-person point of view, the narrator tells someone else's story using *he* or *she*, and *his* or *her*.

PREDICTING /pri dikt′ ing/
Predicting means guessing what will happen next in a text. Predicting includes looking for clues, thinking about what you already know, and asking yourself, "What will happen next?"

PREPOSITION /prep′ə zish′ən/
A preposition is a short connecting word, such as *to, with, from, in,* and *for* that is always followed by a noun or pronoun: *Amy's mother drives her to school. Amy walks back from school with friends.* Prepositions of location tell where something is: *The apple is on the table. The sun is between the mountains. The shoes are under the bed. The bag is next to it.*

PRESENT PROGRESSIVE
/prez′nt prə gres′iv/
A verb in the present progressive describes an action that is happening now: *I am eating my lunch. It is raining today.*

PREVIEWING /prē′vyü′ ing/
Previewing a text is looking at the text to get a general idea about what it contains before reading it more closely. Previewing includes thinking about what you already know about the subject; looking at the title, headings, photographs, and illustrations.

PRONOUN /prō′noun/
A pronoun is a word used instead of a noun, to avoid repeating the noun: *Carlos goes to school. He likes it. He* replaces the proper noun *Carlos; it* replaces the noun *school.*

PROSE /prōz/
Prose is the ordinary form of written language. Most writing that is not poetry, drama (plays), or song is considered prose. Prose is one of the major genres of literature and occurs in fiction and nonfiction.

PUNCTUATION /pungk′chü ā′shən/
Punctuation is the set of signs or marks, such as periods (.) and commas (,), used to divide writing into phrases and sentences, to make their meaning clear. Other punctuation marks indicate questions (?), exclamations (!), pauses (. . .), etc.

RHYME /rīm/
Rhyme is the repetition of sounds at the ends of words. Many poems contain end rhymes, or rhyming words at the ends of lines.

SENTENCE /sen′təns/
A sentence is a group of words with a subject and a verb. A sentence can stand alone.

SETTING /set′ing/
The setting of a literary work is the time and place of the action. The setting includes all the details of a place and time—the year, the time of day, even the weather. The place may be a specific country, state, region, community, neighborhood, building, institution, or home. In most stories, the setting serves as a context in which characters interact. Setting can also help create a feeling, or atmosphere.

SHORT STORY /shôrt stôr′ē/
A short story is a brief work of fiction. Like a novel, a short story presents a sequence of events, or plot. A short story usually communicates a message about life or human nature.

SIMPLE PAST /sim′pəl past/
Verbs in the simple past are used to tell about an action that happened in the past and is completed: *The boy ate the apple. The girl walked up the hill.*

SKIMMING /skim′ing/
Skimming a text is reading it very quickly to gain a general understanding of it. Skimming involves reading the first and second paragraphs quickly, reading only the first sentences of the following paragraphs, and reading the last paragraph quickly.

SONG /sȯng/
A song is a piece of music made especially for singing.

STAGE DIRECTIONS /stāj də rek′shənz/
Stage directions are notes included in a play to describe how the work is to be performed or staged. Stage directions are usually printed in italics and enclosed within parentheses or brackets. Some stage directions describe the movements and costumes, as well as the emotional states and ways of speaking of the characters.

SUMMARIZING /sum′ə rīz′ ing/
Summarizing is restating the main ideas of a text in a shorter form. A way of summarizing is to read a text, reread each paragraph or section, put the text aside, and write the main ideas in one's own words in a sentence or two. Summarizing can help you understand a text better.

SUMMARY /sum′ə rē/
A summary is a brief statement that gives the main points of an event or literary work.

SUPERLATIVE /sə pėr′lə tiv/
A superlative is the form of an adjective or adverb used to compare three or more things. Most one-syllable adjectives and some two-syllable adjectives add *-est* for superlatives: *Biggest* is the superlative form of *big*. Most adjectives of two or more syllables use *the most* for superlatives. (*See also* Comparative.)

SUSPENSE /sə spens′/
Suspense is a feeling of uncertainty about the outcome of events in a literary work. Stories with suspense make the readers ask, "What will happen next?"

TIME PHRASE /tīm frāz/
Time phrases tell the reader when an event happened: *Yesterday, we went to see a movie. Last night, we watched television. Next week, we will go to see my grandmother.*

VERB /vėrb/
A verb is the word or words in a sentence that describe an action, a fact, or a state: *Tom is eating his lunch* (action). *New York has many tall buildings* (fact). *Mary feels sleepy* (state).

VISUALIZING /vizh′ ü ə līz′ ing/
Visualizing means imagining or picturing in your mind the characters, events, and places in a text.

Index

Acknowledgments

Carol Mann Agency. "He Was the Same Age as My Sister" by Mieke C. Malandra, from *I Thought My Father Was God, and Other True Tales,* from NPR's National Story Project, edited and introduced by Paul Auster, 2001. Reprinted by permission of the Carol Mann Agency.

Cinco Puntos Press. "Why Rattlesnake Has Fangs" by Cheryl Giff from *And It Is Still That Way*, collected by Byrd Baylor. Copyright © 1998. Reprinted by permission of Cinco Puntos Press.

Discovery Communications, Inc. "Interview with an Astronaut: Dan Bursch." Copyright © 2000 Discovery Communications, Inc. All rights reserved. www.discovery.com. Reprinted by permission of Discovery Communications, Inc.

Flora Robert, Inc. Excerpt from *The Diary of Anne Frank: The Play* by Frances Goodrich and Albert Hackett, newly adapted by Wendy Kesselman. Copyright © 2001 (revised) the Anne Frank-Fonds, Actors Fund of America, the Dramatists Guild Fund, Inc., New Dramatists. Copyright © 2002, the Anne Frank-Fonds, Actors Fund of America, the Dramatists Guild Fund, Inc., New Dramatists. Used by permission of Flora Robert, Inc.

Harcourt, Inc. "Grass," from *The Complete Poems of Carl Sandburg.* Copyright © 1970, 1969 by Lilian Steichen Sandburg, Trustee. Reprinted by permission of Harcourt, Inc.

HarperCollins Publishers. "Stolen Rope," "The Cookie Jar," and "School Days," from *More True Lies* by George Shannon. Copyright © 1991 by George W. B. Shannon. Used by permission of HarperCollins Publishers.

Hyperion Books. Excerpt from *Lator, Gator* by Laurence Yep. Copyright © 1995 Laurence Yep. Reprinted by permission of Hyperion Books for Children.

Newfront Productions, Inc. "The Case of the Surprise Visitor" and "The Case of the Defaced Sidewalk" by Carol Farley, and "The Case of the Disappearing Signs" by Elizabeth Dearl. Originally appeared on MysteryNet.com Kids Mysteries Site. Copyright © 1996, 2002 Newfront Productions, Inc. Reprinted by permission of Newfront Productions, Inc.

United Feature Syndicate, Inc. Peanuts reprinted by permission of United Feature Syndicate, Inc.

Viking Penguin. Excerpts from *Time Warp Trio: 2095* by Jon Scieszka. Copyright © 1995 by Jon Scieszka. Used by permission of Viking Penguin, an imprint of Penguin Putnam Books for Young Readers, a division of Penguin Putnam, Inc. All rights reserved.

Viking Penguin. Excerpts from *Zlata's Diary* by Zlata Filipović. Copyright © 1994 Editions Robert Laffont/Fixot. Used by permission of Viking Penguin, a division of Penguin Putnam, Inc.

Warner Bros. Publications U.S., Inc. "The Wind Beneath My Wings" by Larry Henley and Jeff Silbar. Copyright © 1982 Warner House of Music and WB Gold Music Corp. All rights reserved. Used by permission of Warner Bros. Publications U.S., Inc., Miami, FL 33014.

Westminster John Knox Press. Excerpt from *A Boat to Nowhere* by Maureen Crane Wartski. Copyright © 1980 Maureen Crane Wartski. Used by permission of Westminster John Knox Press and the author.

Credits